KAGEKI SHOJO!!

The Curtain Rises

story & art by
Kumiko Saiki

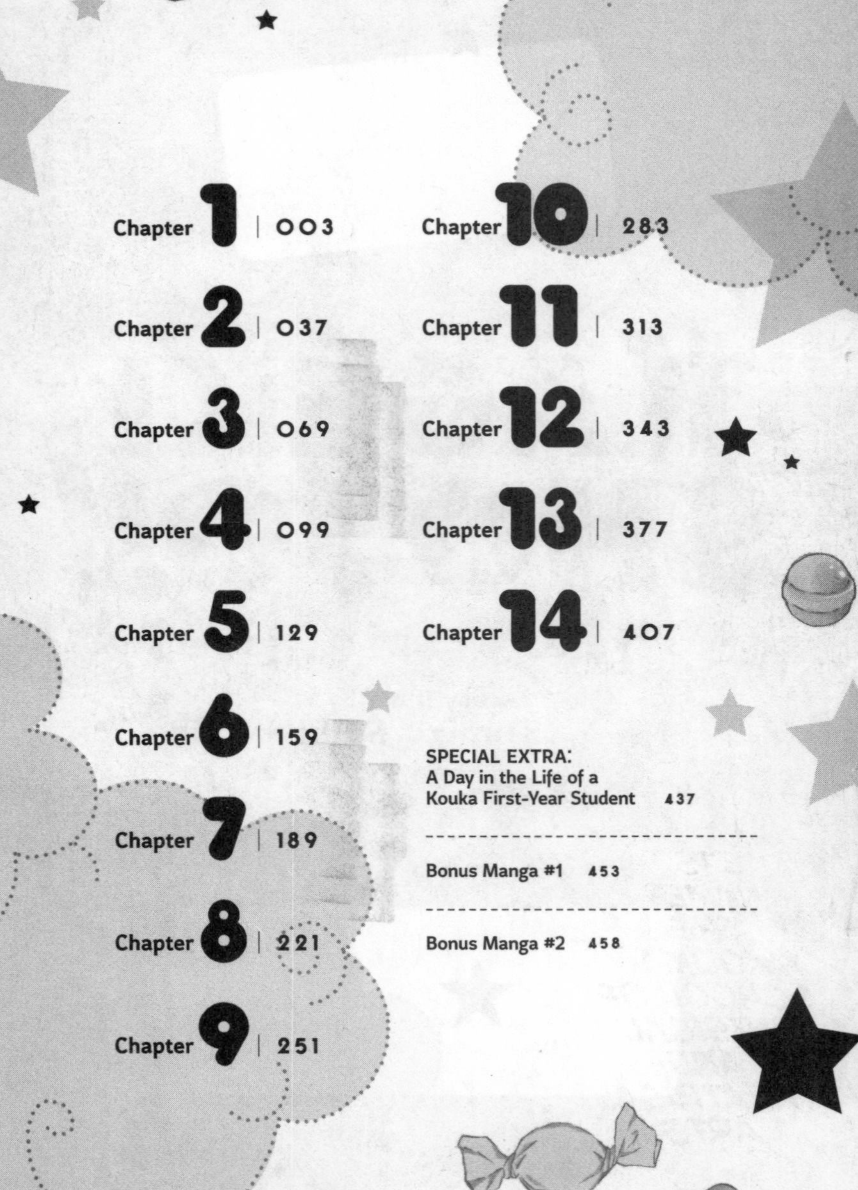

HAVE YOU HEARD ABOUT THE MOST UNIQUE SCHOOL IN THE WHOLE WORLD?
GETTING IN IS AS HARD AS GETTING INTO TOKYO U!
ITS ILLUSTRIOUS ROOTS START WITH ITS FOUNDING AT THE BEGINNING OF THE TAISHO ERA.*
ONLY THE MOST BEAUTIFUL AND DISTINGUISHED YOUNG LADIES ARE ACCEPTED INTO ITS RANKS.
ITS NAME? THE KOUKA SCHOOL OF MUSICAL AND THEATRICAL ARTS.
Chapter 1

1

UNTZ!
UNTZ!
UNTZ!
UNTZ!
UMM?
EXCUSE ME?
TAP
JOLT
HEY!
YOU'RE NARACCHI-SAN, RIGHT? YOU USED TO BE IN JPX!

I KNOW YOU QUIT THE GROUP.
BUT I'M STILL A HUGE FAN!
IT'S TOO BAD THINGS WENT DOWN THE WAY THEY DID!
BUT JUST KEEP YOUR CHIN UP!
AH!
DASH
I'LL BE ROOTING FOR YOU, NARACCHI!
GOOD LUCK!

HAAH!
HAAH!
HAAH!
CRAP!
CRAP!
CRAP!
GROSS!
AI!
WHOA, GIRL!
TMP
WHAT'S UP?

A FANBOY TOUCHED ME.
!
HE DID *WHAT?!*
THAT'S ALL RIGHT

HE TAPPED MY SHOUL-DER.
I'M GLAD THAT'S ALL.
FOR HIS SAKE!

WHERE YOU HEADED, TAICHI?
OH, RIGHT!
MY SISTER SAYS THIS GOT DELIVERED TO HER PLACE.

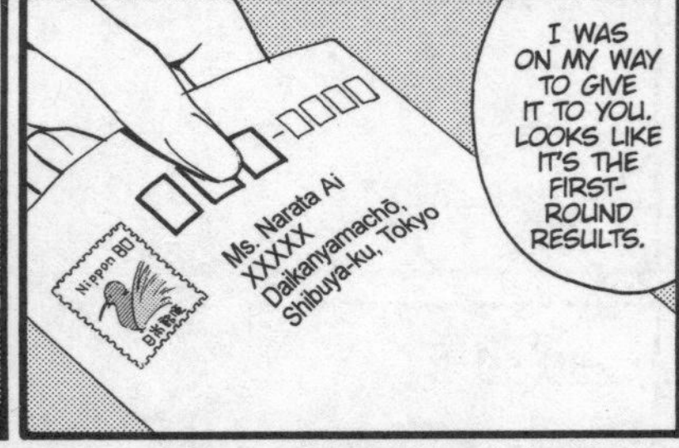
I WAS ON MY WAY TO GIVE IT TO YOU. LOOKS LIKE IT'S THE FIRST-ROUND RESULTS.
Ms. Narata Ai
XXXXX
Daikanyamachō,
Shibuya-ku, Tokyo
Nippon 80

WHOA!
GETTING RIGHT INTO IT!
RIIIP

YOU DID IT!
Ms. Narata Ai
Congratulation
have passed the first round of
dmissions for the Kouka School of
Musical and Theatrical Arts. Please
read the following information
pertaining to the next round
of admission:
March 2012
YEAH. YOU WERE THIRD IN THE JPX ELECTION, RIGHT?
RANK THIRTEEN.
IF I PASS THE NEXT ROUND AND GET ADMITTED...
THEN FOR THE NEXT TWO YEARS...
I'LL LIVE IN A WORLD WITHOUT MEN!
SOME OF THE TEACHERS ARE DUDES.
I'LL DEAL.
I'M A GUY, TOO, YOU KNOW!
YOU DON'T COUNT, TAICHI.

FINGERS CROSSED THAT YOU GET THROUGH THE SECOND ROUND!
NO NEED.
YOU CAN APPLY TO KOUKA AS LONG AS YOU'RE BETWEEN FIFTEEN AND EIGHTEEN YEARS OLD.
SO, EVEN IF I DON'T GET IN THIS YEAR, THEN NEXT YEAR...
I'LL GET IN FOR SURE!

THAT'S TRUE.
SO...
THE NEXT ROUND TAKES PLACE IN KOBE, YEAH?
THAT'S ALL RIGHT
LA LA!
LA LA LA!

FLOWERS...
WITHOUT NAAAMES...
BLOOOOMING IN AN ENDLESS FIELD~!
SARA-SA!
OI, SARASA!
GRAND-PA!!
WHAT ARE YOU SHOUTING ABOUT?!
LOOK!
IT'S HERE!

IT CAME!

THE LETTER FROM KOUKA!

TONK

KYAAAAAA!

CRASH

CLATTER

CRASH

WHAT'S ALL THIS?
WHAT'S GOING ON?
TUNA
YOU KNOW KEN-SAN, WHO RUNS THE TATAMI SHOP? HIS GRANDKID GOT HER RESULTS FROM KOUKA'S FIRST ROUND!
OH, MY!
THAT IS EXCITING!

SARASA-CHAN, WHAT'S THAT?
IF THIS LETTER SAYS I PASSED...
THEN I'M ONE STEP CLOSER TO ATTENDING THE KOUKA SCHOOL OF MUSICAL AND THEATRICAL ARTS!
and Theatrical Arts
〒000-0000
AND WHEN I GRADUATE, I GET TO JOIN THE TROUPE!

I'LL WEAR PRETTY CLOTHES AND SING AND DANCE ALL DAY, EVERY DAY!
ほほー
WOW!

AND I'LL BE ONE STEP CLOSER TO BE-COMING MY BELOVED OSCAR! ♡
KOUKA'S FAMOUS FOR THEIR *ROSE OF VER-SAILLES* PRODUC-TION!
I'VE ALWAYS BEEN AN ANDRÉ STAN MYSELF.

YAY!
I GOTTA SAY, I'M IMPRESSED YOU KNOW WHAT A "STAN" IS, MA'AM!
HA HA HA!
I MAY BE OLD, BUT I'M YOUNG AT HEART!
Sign: Kabayaki
SARASA-CHAN?
ISN'T KOUKA IN KOBE?
WILL YOU BE LIVING IN THE DORMS THERE?
YOUR GRANDPA'S GOING TO MISS YOU!
I KNOW HE'LL BE HAPPY TO SEE YOU BECOME A FAMOUS ACTRESS, BUT STILL...
KEN-SAN'S GOING TO MISS YOU!
OH.
HEY! SARASA!!
OPEN THE DAMN LETTER ALREADY!!
YOU'RE GETTING ON MY LAST NERVE!

YOUR DEAD GRANDMA DREAMED OF GOIN' TO KOUKA!
RAR!
YOU SURE AS HELL BETTER GET IN!!

RIIIP
Nippon 80
Watanabe Sarasa
XXXX XXX,
Taitō-ku Toky

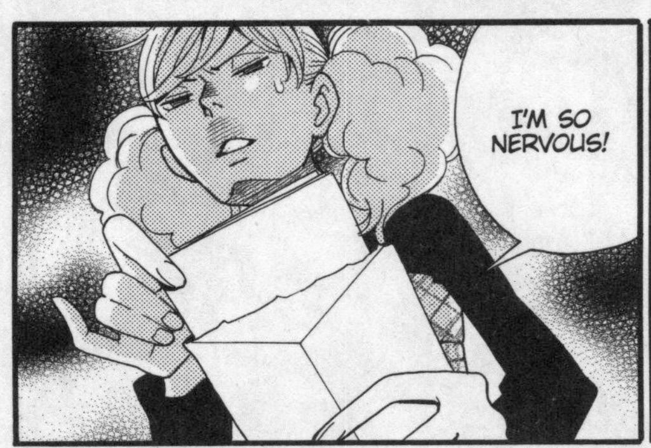
I'M SO NERVOUS!

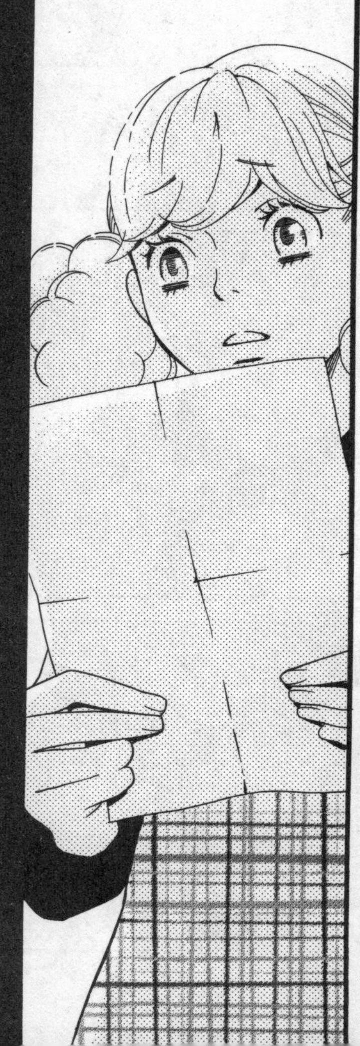
THE KOUKA ACTING TROUPE...

WAS FOUNDED IN THE TAISHO ERA.
IT WAS STARTED BY DIRECTOR OOIZUMI MINORU, WHO WAS PART OF A GROUP OF BIG-NAME CORPORATIONS IN KOBE.

THE ALL-FEMALE TROUPE WAS COMPRISED OF YOUNG, UNMARRIED WOMEN.

THEIR EXTRAVAGANT, GORGEOUS PRODUCTIONS STOLE THE HEARTS OF EVERYONE WHO SAW THEM.
TEN YEARS AFTER ITS FOUNDING, THE KOUKA THEATER OPENED ADMISSIONS TO THE PUBLIC.

AS THEIR POPULARITY EXPLODED, THEY OPENED A SECOND THEATER IN TOKYO.
THEIR OTOKOYAKU, OR MALE ROLES, PLAYED BY ACTRESSES FAR MORE HANDSOME AND CHARMING THAN ANY GUY, WON MANY FEMALE FANS' HEARTS.
THE KOUKA TROUPE PERFORMANCES WERE SPLIT INTO FOUR GROUPS: THE SPRING, SUMMER, AUTUMN, AND WINTER TROUPES, WHO PERFORMED YEAR-ROUND.
FINALLY, THE GROUP OPENED THE KOUKA SCHOOL OF MUSICAL AND THEATRICAL ARTS, DESIGNED TO HELP DISCOVER THE TROUPE'S NEXT BIG STARS. THOUGH MANY YOUNG LADIES DREAM OF WALKING ITS VENERATED HALLS, ONLY FOUR PERCENT OF APPLICANTS MAKE THE CUT.

NOW, IN THE SPRING OF ITS CENTENNIAL YEAR...
Kouka School of Musical and Theatrical Arts
Second Admissions Round

HOW MANY APPLICANTS DID WE GET IN TOTAL?
EXACTLY 1,135.
THESE ARE THE TOP 200.
HERE A WHOLE HOUR BEFORE THE TEST STARTS, TOO! HARD-WORKING GIRLS.
S.H. OMEGA
IT'S THE SAME STORY EVERY YEAR... BUT NOBLE NONETHELESS.
GOING HERE MIGHT BE THEIR DREAM, BUT THEY'LL SOON FIND THE PECKING ORDER A NIGHTMARE.
THEY ALREADY KNOW ABOUT THAT NIGHTMARE, MAN.
OH!

HEE HEE!
I KNEW IT! AI'S THE CUTEST ONE HERE! ♡
AH, RIGHT. YOUR PRECIOUS NIECE. WHERE ARE HER PARENTS?
I'M HERE FOR HER INSTEAD!
OH. THAT'S BORING.
THERE'S HAKUHO MIYUKI! SHE WAS A MUSUMEYAKU IN THE FLOWER TROUPE WAY BACK WHEN.
GUESS THAT'S HER DAUGHTER.
I'VE SEEN HER AT A FEW ENTRANCE CEREMONIES OVER THE YEARS.
IF SHE GETS IN, THAT'LL MAKE THREE GENERATIONS FROM THAT FAMILY TO GET INTO KOUKA.
THAT ONE'S THE DAUGHTER OF THAT TOKYO BALLET SCHOOL DIRECTOR, RIGHT?
SHE'S GOT THE HIGHEST SCORE OUT OF EVERYONE SO FAR.
SHE'S IN FOR SURE.
HOLY MOLY! ARE THOSE TWINS?!
HERE I WAS THINKING, "WHY'S THE SAME GIRL TAKIN' THE TEST TWICE?!"
ARE YOU SERIOUS?
EVERY-ONE'S SO THIN!
WORRY
WORRY
HMMMM.
WHAT?

SOMEONE MISSING?
REMEMBER THAT WEIRD GIRL?

MAYBE SHE DIDN'T PASS.
MAYBE.

MURMUR
LOOK! THAT'S HER!
THE GIRL WHO USED TO BE IN JPX! NARATA AI!
WHAT?! YOU MEAN THE IDOL THAT GOT TOTALLY CANCELED? THE ONE WHO WAS FORCED TO LEAVE THE GROUP?
SHE'S *THAT* NARACCHI?!

WAIT, WHAT HAPPENED?

YOU DON'T KNOW?!

IT HAPPENED AT A HANDSHAKE EVENT WITH A FAN.

WORD GOT OUT TO THE REST OF THE GROUP'S FANS.

Anonymous
naracchi fans long have we waited

Anonymous
lmao where's the lie though? you guys ARE creep

Anonymous
Haven't seen Naracchi in a w

An seen how
I she's ever

mous
fired Imao

AND THEY GOT ALL BUTT-HURT, SO SHE WAS FIRED!

Anonymous
Poor Naracchi

SO, WHY'S SHE GOING FOR KOUKA?
DUNNO. MAYBE SHE HAD AN IN?

I MEAN, NARACCHI'S MOM IS A MOVIE STAR WHO'S ONLY FAMOUS FOR GETTING NAKED.
OH, NARATA KIMIKO, RIGHT?

WHAT-EVER.
I'M USED TO THIS.

WHEN YOU'RE AN IDOL, YOU GET USED TO STRANGERS...
TALKING ABOUT YOU.

I DIDN'T GO TO HIGH SCHOOL, SO I JUST WORE MY MIDDLE SCHOOL UNIFORM.
I BET I LOOK STUPID.
WHAT NUMBER WAS I AGAIN?
I'VE NEVER HAD ANY FRIENDS, ANYWAY.
FLUTTER

012 Kouka School of Musical and Theatrical Arts
Second Admission Round
Admission Form

Number:	0087
Name:	Narata Ai

Please arrive at the testing lo
by no later than 9 A.M.
Do not forget to bring this form with

OH!
HEY, NARATA!
YOUR CUTE NIECE IS GETTING CLOSE TO THE KOUKA CHERRY TREE.
CRAP!
WAUGH!
I FORGOT TO WARN HER!
HEH HEH! TOO LATE!
SHE'S ALREADY UNDER THE BLOSSOMS.
IT'S SO PRET-TY.
WHERE IS EVERY-ONE?
YOU'D THINK THEY'D ALL COME TO CHECK IT OUT.

WOW!!
I CAN'T BELIEVE IT!
THIS IS AWESOME!
HEY! YOU THERE! EXCUSE ME!
GRK!
COULD YOU TAKE A PIC OF ME?!

UGH. REALLY?
EW! A FAN-GIRL.
HA HA! THERE GOES ANOTHER!
OH! IT'S THE WEIRD GIRL!
SORRY, AI.
HYUUU
!!
FWISH

FWOOSH
EEEEK!

LOOK AT THOSE LEGS!
THEY'RE AS LONG AS A GIRAFFE'S!
HER EYES ARE SPARK-LING...
LIKE THEY'RE FILLED WITH STARS.
HI THERE!
AND...
I'M WATA-NABE SARASA, AND I'M FIFTEEN!

SHE WAS...
TERRIFYINGLY...
TALL.

AH!
HEY, YOUR ADMISSION PAPER WENT FLYING.
IT'S UP IN THE TREE.
I'LL GET IT FOR YOU!
HUP!
FWP
HUH?
THIS GIRL ...!

IS SHE FLOAT-ING?
NO, THAT'S NOT IT.
THERE!
SHE JUMPED WITHOUT USING HER KNEES...
THEN LANDED SMOOTHLY.
HER CORE STRENGTH MUST BE INCREDIBLE!
HERE YA GO!
AS THANKS, COULD YOU TAKE MY PICTURE? ♡

THANKS SO MUCH!
I'M DOING WHAT NOW?
WAIT...
I'VE NEVER SEEN A CHERRY TREE THIS BIG OR BEAUTIFUL!
I WANNA SEND A PICTURE OF IT AND ME TO MY GRANDPA! HE'S BUSY WORKING TODAY!
TAKE...
A PICTURE?

UGH!
THOSE GIRLS MUST NOT KNOW THE URBAN LEGEND.
"WHOMEVER STANDS UNDER THE KOUKA CHERRY TREE BEFORE BEING ADMITTED..."
"WILL NEVER MAKE IT TO THE TOP." OR SO THE LEGEND GOES.
OH, AI.
GUESS THOSE TWO ARE DOOMED!
TAKING IT NOW.
READY?

THIS ...
WAS HOW I MET...
WATANABE SARASA.
KA-SNAP

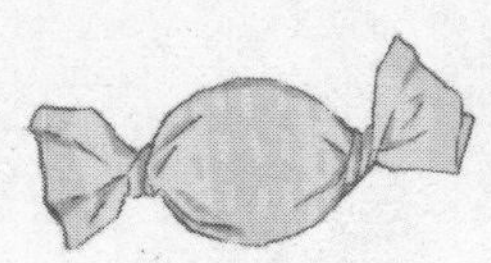

KAGEKI SHOJO!!

The Curtain Rises

2

WE WILL NOW PRESENT THE ADMISSION RESULTS...
FOR THE 100TH CLASS OF THE KOUKA SCHOOL FOR MUSICAL AND THEATRICAL ARTS!
TODAY IS THE DAY WE FIND OUT...
紅華歌劇音楽学校
1114 1086 0097
0593 0089 1874
0073 1117 0351 0050 0719
0954 0377 1011 0482 0075
0744 0087 0071 0389 0174
0021 0917 0598 0474
0883 1111 0558 0467
1012 0553 0042 0703 0251
Sign: Students Admitted
IF WE GOT IN OR NOT.
HERE ARE THE ADMITTED STUDENTS!
TODAY, I'M MORE CONCERNED WITH NOT STANDING OUT...
THAN WHETHER OR NOT I GOT IN.

THOSE SUNGLASSES GIVE YOU BIG DAIMON FORCE VIBES.

I DON'T EVEN KNOW WHAT THAT IS.
IT'S FROM THIS COP SHOW CALLED *SEIBU KEISATSU*. IT'S OLDER THAN BOTH OF US.

TAICHI, DID YOU SEE THE RESULTS?

HOW FAR DOWN THE LIST...
WAS MY NUMBER?
THERE ARE TONS OF CAMERAS HERE, AND IF I GO CHECK FOR MYSELF, IT'LL CAUSE A SCENE.

YOU'RE ASSUMING YOU GOT IN?
THAT'S PRETTY BOLD.
THERE'S *NO WAY* I DIDN'T GET IN.
I MEAN...

A ROTTEN FISH IS STILL A FISH!
YOU'RE NOT ROTTEN, AI.
キリッ
SHING
YOUR OPINION COUNTS FOR SQUAT.

YOU WERE IN THE MIDDLE. TAKE THAT, MISS HIGH-AND-MIGHTY!
GOD, YOU'RE SO IMMATURE, TAICHI.

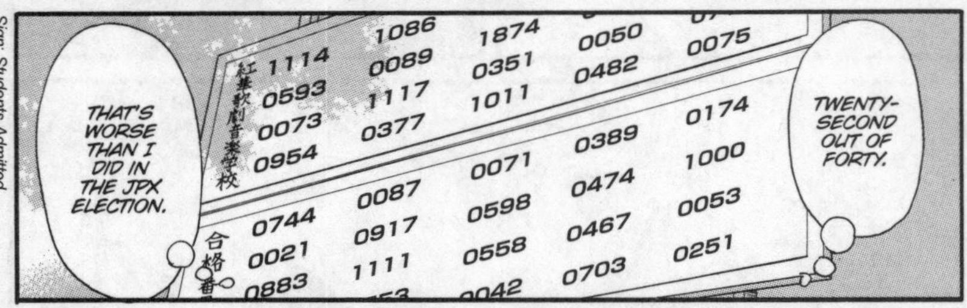

Sign: Students Admitted

......

WHAT ABOUT HER?

THAT GIRL...

DID SHE GET IN?

I KIND OF HOPE...
SHE DIDN'T.

HYPER PEOPLE LIKE HER...
ANNOY ME.

OH MY GOSH !!

HELLO, GRANDPA?! I'M IN!
I WAS RIGHT THERE AT THE VERY END!
FLIP
I'M JUST GOING TO KEEP MY DISTANCE.
I DID IT, MOM!
THERE I AM!
OH, HONEY. THERE'S ALWAYS NEXT YEAR.
SWEETIE?
I GOT IN!
KYAA!
FLAIL
FLAIL
KYAA!
O.M.G!
THIS WAS MY LAST CHANCE...!
I TRIED SO DAMN HARD!
WHY...?
LADIES!

WOULD THOSE OF YOU WHO HAVE BEEN ADMITTED PLEASE PRO-CEED TO THE RECEPTION HALL?
STEP
OUR CONDOLENCES TO ALL THOSE NOT ADMITTED THIS YEAR.
PLEASE LEAVE THE SCHOOL GROUNDS AS SOON AS YOU ARE ABLE.
C'MON.
LET'S GO, AI.

HISS
SO, YOU CHEAT-ED YOUR WAY IN?

DON'T LISTEN TO HER.
PETTY GIRLS LIKE HER COULD NEVER MAKE IT INTO KOUKA.
I'M FINE.

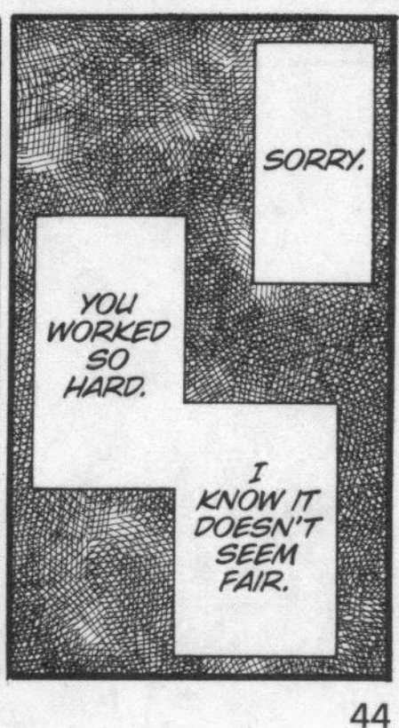
SORRY.
YOU WORKED SO HARD.
I KNOW IT DOESN'T SEEM FAIR.

OH, NARATA-SENSEI! ANOTHER TEACHER WAS LOOKING FOR YOU.
HUH?
IS THAT NARAC-CHI?!
HUH?!
WHA?!
SHE'S YOUR NIECE?
WHAT?! NO WAY!
HOW-EVER ...

I HAVE SOMETHING THAT YOU DON'T.
SOMETHING IMPORTANT.
SO YOU SEE, THAT'S WHY I'D LIKE TO SIT IN THE PARENT SECTION TODAY!
WOULD THAT BE ALL RIGHT?
TEE HEE!
I MEAN... WE CAN'T STOP YOU.
SOMETHING THE KOUKA TROUPE PRIZES MORE THAN ANYTHING.

THAT THING ...
SHE'S FROM JPX!
WOW!
CHATTER
IS STA--
SORRY, Y'ALL!
!!

I HAD TO CALL SOMEONE TO SHARE THE GOOD NEWS, AND IT ENDED UP TAKING FOREVER!
YOU HAVEN'T STARTED WITHOUT ME, RIGHT?!
HUH? WAIT, AREN'T YOU...
SHWP
MURMUR
OH MY GOSH, YOU GOT IN, TOO?! WE'RE GONNA BE CLASS-MATES!
I'M SARASA! OH, BUT I ALREADY TOLD YOU THAT!

WHAT'S YOUR NAME?
GRIN

HMPH!

WHY DON'T YOU TAKE A SEAT?
OH, YOU'RE THE BALLET TEACHER!
LOOKING AS PRINCELY AS EVER!
HA! THANKS ...?

WHERE ARE YOUR FOLKS? DID YOU COME ALONE?
YUP!
EVERY-ONE, PLEASE TAKE YOUR SEATS.

SHE DIDN'T RECOGNIZE A FORMER IDOL?
MAYBE SHE'S AN ALIEN.
OR MAYBE ...
SHE'S DOING IT ON PURPOSE?
YOU KNOW SHE CAN HEAR YOU.
UGH.
TUMP
WHAT THE HELL...
IS WRONG WITH HER?
CLENCH

WHO THE HELL IS THAT GIRL?!
CONGRATU-LATIONS ON YOUR ADMIT-TANCE.
BUT GETTING IN IS ONLY THE FIRST STEP.
ボ SZZ
ボ SZZ
ボ SZZ
ボ SZZ
HEY, DON'T PLAY WITH YOUR FOOD!
SLUUUMP
WHAT'S WITH THE GRUMPY FACE?
YOU GOT IN!

AREN'T YOU HAPPY?

I AM. KNOW WHAT MAKES ME TRULY ECSTATIC?

LIVING IN A WORLD WITHOUT MEN.

SO.

THAT GIRL, SARASA.

OH, YES, HER.

HA HA!

HOW THE HELL...

DID SHE GET IN?

IS IT JUST BECAUSE SHE'S TALL OR SOME-THING?

IT'S NOT LIKE YOU TO BE SO INTERESTED IN OTHERS.
SHE WAS IN MY GROUP DURING THE BALLET AUDITION.
POSE
BOMP
↓↓↑+K
HER MOVEMENTS WERE ROUGH AND WILD, HARDLY GRACEFUL AT ALL.
THERE WERE PLENTY OF GIRLS WHO WERE WAY BETTER DANCERS THAN HER.
SHE'S ONLY BEEN TAKING BALLET CLASSES FOR HALF A YEAR, ALL TO GET READY FOR THE AUDITION.
I HEARD SHE DIDN'T DO SO HOT DURING VOICE AUDITIONS, EITHER.
BUT SHE STUMBLED THROUGH TO THE INTERVIEW, AND THAT'S WHERE SHE CLINCHED IT.
THOUGH THE VOTE ON HER *WAS* SPLIT.

THEATER PROFES-SOR ANDOU-SENSEI...

AND HISTORY PROFESSOR OHKI-SENSEI BOTH LIKED HER.

Where's the fun in admitting the same students we always have?
It's our centennial year!
It's the perfect opportunity to be a bit daring.

I agree with Andou-sensei.
The most impor-tant quality a pro-spective Kouka member can have....
is **star quality!**

Our shows revolve around the leads. Our top performers need something **extra.**
Remember the faces of those girls during auditions?
They were all smiling, but could barely hide how nervous they felt.
Next up, 0251.
BLESSED WITH INCREDIBLE HEIGHT...
BUT THAT GIRL ...
Yes, sir!
Number 0251, Watanabe Sarasa, ready to go!
AND THOSE LONG ARMS AND LEGS...

HER CHEEKS WERE FLUSHED WITH EXCITEMENT.
Thank you for having me today!
HER EYES SPARKLING WITH HOPE.
WHAT DO YOU THINK OF HER?
SHE WAS NO BALLERINA.
BUT...
HER BODY MOVED SO SMOOTHLY AND PRECISELY.
THAT'S NOT JUST SOMETHING YOU'RE BORN WITH, EITHER.
HOW DO YOU THINK...
SHE GOT THAT WAY?

I REALLY DON'T CARE.
MAYBE SHE JUST HAD A REALLY GOOD HOME ENVIRONMENT OR SOMETHING.

I DUNNO.

......

I HEARD SHE JUST LIVES ALONE WITH HER GRANDPA.

NOT GOING BACK TO TOKYO?

NOPE.

Cheraton

I FIGURED I'D GET IN...

SO, I PACKED UP ALL MY STUFF.

COULD YOU SEND IT HERE WHEN YOU GO TO TOKYO?

I'M GOING TO STAY AT THE HOTEL.
I HAVE NO DESIRE TO GO BACK *THERE.*

Cancel

Hey mom, I got admitted to Kouka. Dunno if you actually care

Cancel Draft Send

Cc/Bcc:

Subject: I'm in Kobe

Hey mom, I got admitted to Kouka.

"I HEARD SHE JUST LIVES ALONE WITH HER GRANDPA."

Delete Draft

Save Draft

Cancel

BUT SHE STOPPED EVERY FIVE SECONDS TO REPLY TO TEXTS.
SHE GOT ALL EXCITED ABOUT "RUSHING BACK TO TOKYO."

THAT GIRL...

VOOM
I GOTTA CATCH THE BULLET TRAIN!

REPLY.

VA-VOOM
GOTTA HURRY!

REPLY.

WHAT A WEIRDO! JUST REPLY TO EVERY-THING LATER.

Kouka Student Dorm

NEW STUDENT?
WHAT'S YOUR NAME?

NARATA AI.

I THINK I'VE SEEN YOU ON TV...
OH, SORRY, DEAR! FORGET I SAID ANYTHING.
IT'S FINE.

THE PREP STUDENTS' ROOMS ARE IN THE SECOND BUILDING ON THE THIRD AND FOURTH FLOORS.

YOU'LL BE IN A DOUBLE, ROOM 302.

I DON'T SMELL THE STINK OF MEN HERE AT ALL!

I FEEL SO AT EASE.

A BLESSED...
ANXIETY-FREE LIFE.
MITCHELL
O.M.G!! ♡
SLAM
バタン

?
YOU WANT TO CHANGE ROOMS?
I'M SORRY, DEAR, BUT NOBODY GETS SPECIAL TREATMENT HERE.
SCREECH
VROOOOOOM
A.R. HOME FURNISHINGS
R. HOME FURNISHINGS

OH! YOU'RE BACK!
ガシャーン
CLATTER
ガシャン
CLATTER
ガシャン
CLATTER
ガシャン
CLATTER
UH?
UMM?
MITCHELL
NONO JILL

WHAT'S THIS SUPPOSED TO BE?
MITCHELL
NONO JILL
I...
REALLY NEED MY PRIVACY.
SHK
シャッ
OH! BY THE WAY, MY NAME'S--
I KNOW!!
OH, RIGHT! WHAT WAS YOUR NAME AGAIN?
......

OH, YEAH! NARATA AI!!
IT'S HERE ON THE ROOMMATE SHEET!
NARATA'S A COOL NAME!
CAN I CALL YOU AI-CHAN?
DID YOU NOT HAVE A TV AT HOME?!
MITCHELL
OF COURSE I HAD A TV!
MY GRANDPA AND I LOVE TO WATCH PERIOD DRAMAS!
OH, I LOVED YOUR SUNGLASSES THE OTHER DAY! YOU LOOKED SOOOO COOL! LIKE THE DAIMON FORCE!
?
BUT Y'KNOW WHAT SHOW I'M INTO RIGHT NOW?
SHADOW WARRIORS! IT'S SOOO GOOD!
SHWOOP
ニョキーッ
MITCHELL
NONO JILL

BEST GUY IS HATTORI HANZO, HANDS DOWN.
WHAT THE HELL ...
IS HER DEAL ?!
DON'T VIOLATE MY BORDER!
VIOLATE YOUR WHAT?
OH, ARE YOU WORRIED ABOUT VIOLENCE? THE SHOW'S NOT THAT BAD, DON'T WORRY! ♡
STAY ON YOUR SIDE!
AWW!
I CAN'T HELP IT! I'M TOO TALL TO STRETCH OUT ON MY SIDE OF THE FLOOR!
THEN DON'T STRETCH OUT ON THE FLOOR!
AWWWWW!
TAP
LET'S KIOSK
HA HA!
WOW!

THEY'VE GOT NOTHING BETTER TO REPORT ON?
TOMOR-ROW...
JPX48
NARACCHI AT KOUKA?!
HEE HEE! I CAN'T WAIT TO SPEND THE NEXT TWO YEARS WITH YOU!
MY LIFE IN THE WORLD OF THEATER...
ROLL
AI-CHAN! ♡
TWO YEARS...?!
!!
AW! DON'T IGNORE ME, AI-CHAN!
FINALLY BEGINS.
MITCHELL
NONO JILL

3

BEFORE NEW STUDENTS START AT KOUKA...
THEY MUST GO THROUGH GUID-ANCE WEEK.
IT'S A WEEK FULL OF SESSIONS THAT HELP STUDENTS SETTLE IN AT KOUKA.
BUT...
IT'S MORE LIKE A DRY RUN OF CLASSES BEFORE THEY START IN EARNEST.
ZZZ!
ZZZ!

SO ANNOYING!
OH?
GOOD MORNING, NARATA-SAN.
HELLO.
WHERE'S WATANABE-SAN?
WHO CARES?
IT'S A SEVEN-MINUTE WALK FROM THE DORMS TO CAMPUS.
TODAY'S THE LAST DAY OF GUIDANCE WEEK, HUH?
YESTERDAY WE FINISHED UP WITH MUSIC.
AND WE'RE DONE WITH LIFESTYLE AND HEALTH, TOO.
WHAT DO YOU THINK WE'LL DO TODAY?
OH, GOD, SPEAKING OF MUSIC, DID YOU HEAR WATANABE-SAN YESTERDAY?

CAN YOU BELIEVE SHE CAN'T PLAY PIANO?!

I DIDN'T THINK YOU COULD GET IN HERE WITHOUT *THAT!*

WHEN WE WERE DOING SOLFEGE*, WATANABE-SAN WAS, LIKE...

*Solfege is the "do-re-mi" system of reading musical notes.

Solfege? What's that?

Sounds like a yummy dessert!

I BET IT'S FLUFFY!

SHE THOUGHT "CONCONE*" WAS A TYPE OF PASTRY.

IS FOOD ALL SHE THINKS ABOUT?

SHE SAID THAT CHORÜBUNGEN* WAS "STRAIGHT OUT OF A VIDEO GAME."

HA!

*Giuseppe Concone was an Italian vocal teacher.

*Chorübungen is a famous vocal exercise.

......

DID SOMEONE LIKE HER GET INTO KOUKA?

HOW ...

EVERY-ONE...

I KNOW, RIGHT?

IS THINKING THE SAME THING.

GOOD MORNING, EVERYONE!
AM I THE FIRST ONE HERE?

EH?

WHAT ?!

YOU'RE LATE. A HALF HOUR LATE, IN FACT.

HUH?! BUT I CAME AT THE SAME TIME AS YESTERDAY!
AND YESTERDAY, WE TOLD YOU TO BE HERE A HALF HOUR EARLY.
YOU NEED TO PAY BETTER ATTENTION.
WHAT A MEAN TRICK TO PULL ON THE LAST DAY!
AI-CHAN, YOU DIDN'T WAKE ME UP!
IGNORE.
EVERYONE'S WAITING. LINE UP.
RIGHT THEN!
TODAY'S YOUR LAST DAY OF GUID-ANCE WEEK.
WE'LL BE DOING A GROUP ACTIVITY!

IT'S A BASIC TRAINING EXERCISE USED IN THE JSDF.
YOU'LL BE LED BY MEMBERS OF THE ITAMI MILITARY BASE SECURITY FORCE.

MODERN DANCE.
BALLET.
MUSIC.
TRADI-TIONAL DANCE.
CLASSICAL THEATER.
AND THE JSDF?!

MY NAME IS ANAI ICHII. CONGRAT-ULATIONS ON YOUR ACCEP-TANCE.
TODAY, I'LL BE TEACHING YOU ALL ABOUT WORKING AS A GROUP.
WORKING TOGETHER WITH YOUR COMRADES--OR YOUR CO-STARS--IS A VITAL SKILL.
SNAP
FORM FOUR GROUPS OF TEN!
ARE YOU READY, RECRUITS?!
Y-YES, SIR.
I CAN'T HEAR YOU!
YES, SIR!!
...
NARATA AND THE VICE PRINCI-PAL?
WHAT'S EVERYONE WATCH-ING?
ANDOU-KUN, COME LOOK!
OH MY GOSH, CAPTAIN ANAI!!
I FORGOT IT WAS THE LAST DAY OF GUIDANCE WEEK!

GOD, HE'S SUCH A CHARACTER! I LOVE HIM!
SAME!
A WONDERFUL MAN, INDEED.
I THOUGHT GUIDANCE WEEK WAS SUPPOSED TO BE OVER BY NOW?
OH, YEAH. IT'S NOON ALREADY.
WELL...
THERE'S ONE GROUP WHO JUST CAN'T GET IT RIGHT.
THE UPPERCLASSMEN'S OPINION IS THAT IF ONE GROUP HAS TO STAY, EVERY GROUP HAS TO STAY.
THEIR CLASSMATES DON'T SEEM TOO HAPPY ABOUT THAT.
ATTENTION!
SIXTY PACES!
ARM TO THE RIGHT--
SPREAD OUT!!
SHWIP
GYAH!
H-HEY!

THIS IS, LIKE, THE **HUNDREDTH** TIME YOU'VE WHACKED ME! ARE YOU DOING IT ON PURPOSE?!

S-SORRY! I DIDN'T MEAN TO, I JUST HAVE REALLY LONG ARMS.

SHAKE オロ
オロ SHAKE

NOW YOU'RE BRAG-GING?!

HEY! YOU TWO!

STOP!
RIGHT NOW!

OKAY, LET'S DO IT AGAIN!
SPREAD OUT SO YOUR HANDS ARE JUST BARELY ABOUT TO TOUCH YOUR NEIGHBOR'S SHOULDER!
YES, SIR!

SALUTE!
FWIP
FACE RIGHT!
ONE!
TWO!
TMP
SOL-DIERS, MARCH!
LEFT FOOT!
TMP TMP TMP
ONE, TWO!
ONE, TWO!
SOL-DIERS, TURN RIGHT!
TMP TMP
ONE, TWO!
ONE, TWO!
TMP
HMMM.
SOME-THING'S OFF.
He sounds just like Anago!
From "Sazae-san"!
KYA! KYA! KYA!

HELLO THERE, ANDOU-SENSEI, NARATA-SENSEI, MR. VICE PRINCIPAL!
HEY.
HUH?
WHAT ARE YOU ALL DOING HERE?
IT'S OUR LUNCH BREAK!
WE CAME TO SEE CAPTAIN ANAGO!
POPULAR GUY.
HIM, AND...
NARACCHI.
SHE'S JUST TRYING TO LIVE LIFE AS A REGULAR STUDENT.
OH, WE KNOW, NARATA-SENSEI!
BUT WE CAN'T HELP BUT BE CURIOUS!
AFTER ALL...

SHE'S ALREADY GOT SO MUCH EXPERIENCE.
SHE'S STOOD ON BIGGER STAGES THAN MOST OF US EVER WILL.
BUT SHE REALLY DOES SEEM LIKE A NORMAL GIRL.
SHE'S GOT SKILLS, THOUGH. EASILY THE BEST OF THE NEWBIES.
THOUGH IN JPX, SHE ALWAYS SEEMED TO FADE INTO THE BACKGROUND.
HMM. I HAVE AN IDEA.
YOU AND...
YOU.
AND YOU TWO, STEP OUT.
THERE! THE FOUR OF YOU, TRY THAT AGAIN.

SALUTE!
FWIP
AT EASE!
FWIP
FWIP
ATTENTION!
ARM RIGHT, LINE UP!
SHOVE

!

I SHOVED HER PRETTY HARD...
BUT SHE DIDN'T EVEN BUDGE!
OKAY, THAT'S ENOUGH!

YOU, YOU'RE ABOUT A SECOND OFF FROM EVERYONE ELSE.
DON'T WORRY ABOUT THE OTHERS. MOVE ON COMMAND AND TRUST THEY WILL, TOO.
YOU. YOU'RE VERY CRITICAL.
THAT'S NOT ALWAYS A BAD THING.
YOU...
BUT KNOW WHEN TO EASE UP.

WAIT, SHE WAS IN JPX?!
IS THE CAPTAIN A FANBOY?
YOUR TIMING IS GOOD.
BUT YOUR CORE IS A BIT WEAK.
THIS IS ABOUT TEAM-WORK.
EVEN IF YOU'RE DOING IT PERFECTLY, YOU NEED TO ADJUST TO FIT THOSE AROUND YOU.
THOUGH I HAVE TO SAY, I THOUGHT YOU'D BE SOMEWHAT USED TO DOING SO ALREADY.
NO MATTER.
JPX'S DANCE ROUTINES WERE ABOUT AS RIGOROUS AS SOMETHING YOU'D SEE IN A SCHOOL TALENT SHOW.
THEY DIDN'T REQUIRE THIS LEVEL OF PERFEC-TION.

JPX48...
IT IS, AS YOU KNOW, AN IDOL GROUP.
THE PRODUCERS TOLD US THAT ONLY THE FEW GIRLS WHO ACHIEVED "PERFECTION"...
WOULD GET ANY LOVE AND AFFECTION FROM THE PUBLIC.
SO, ME AND THE OTHER MEM-BERS...
WORKED OUR BUTTS OFF.

AND STILL THE FANS DEMANDED MORE.
THOUGH ...
I CAN'T SPEAK...
FOR EVERY-ONE ELSE.
ONLY ME.
AI-CHAN, YOU'RE SO COOL! ♡
BUT WHY DO YOU KNOW SO MUCH ABOUT JPX?
SO ANNOY-ING!

I... I SEE.

AWW!

HE'S CRYING!

KYA! KYA!

SO, YOU J-IDOLS ARE PROFESSIONALS, TOO.

I'M SORRY TO INSULT YOU.

MY LITTLE ONE'S A BIG FAN, ACTUALLY.

スゥ SLIIIDE

WHOOSH

PARDON ME.
BUT I DON'T LIKE BEING TOUCHED.

BOY, I JUST DON'T GET GIRLS NOWA-DAYS.
MY OLDEST DAUGHTER WON'T EVEN HUG ME ANYMORE!
PFFF! HE'S TALKING ABOUT HIS FAMILY!
EEEK! POOR PAPA!
WELL, SOME PEOPLE WILL TAKE OFFENSE TO ANYTHING, I GUESS.
RIGHT, THEN! NEXT.
HOLY HELL, YOU'RE TALL FOR A BROAD!
AND THAT'S SEXUAL HARASS-MENT, SIR!
IT'S WHAT?!
I SWEAR, THE WORLD'S HARDER TO LIVE IN EVERY DAY!
RIGHT. THEN, WHAT YOU NEED TO WORK ON...

NOTHING, ACTUALLY.

\(^o^)/

YAAAAAAY!♡

HOWEVER! BECAUSE YOU'RE SO DAMN TALL...

THIS ISN'T HARASSMENT, NOW, YOU SEE?

YOUR ARMS AND LEGS ARE LONGER THAN YOUR COMRADES'.

AS SUCH, YOU NEED TO TAKE OTHERS INTO CONSIDERATION!

WOULD IT BE ALL RIGHT IF I GAVE YOUR SHOULDER A SHOVE?

?

SURE?

SHOVE

WOBBLE
ヨ
ロ
ッ
GOOD!
YOU'VE GOT STRONG LEGS AND A GOOD CORE!
HMM!
JUST AS I EXPECTED.

NOW, THEN--

HOLD ON, SIR!

SPIN

ARE YOU GOING TO COMPLAIN ABOUT SEXUAL HARASSMENT AGAIN?

NO! BUT THAT SHOVE JUST NOW WAS A CHEAP SHOT!

HNNNNNG!

WHAM

THIS ISN'T THE TIME FOR GAMES.
BUT FINE.
GRAB
HAH!
EH?
HNNNG!
SMIRK
I WON'T MOVE AN INCH FROM THIS SPOT!
HMM.
INCREDIBLE.

HOW'D YOU LIKE TO JOIN THE JSDF?
NO, THANKS! I CAN'T BE OSCAR IN THE JSDF!

SURE YOU CAN!
OSCAR'S A BRIGADIER, AFTER ALL!
YOU COULD BE SOME-THIN' LIKE THAT.
THE CAP KNOWS ROV?!

REALLY ...?!
トゥクン
BA-THUMP
SHE'S CONSIDERING IT?!

NO, I THINK I'LL PASS.
I WANT TO STUDY HERE AND LEARN AS MUCH AS I CAN...

AFTER ALL, I CAME HERE TO LEARN HOW TO BE THE OSCAR OF MY DREAMS!
PFFT!
HEY, WATANABE! DO YOU KNOW WHAT IT MEANS TO BE OSCAR?!
IF YOU WANNA BE OSCAR...

YOU'VE GOTTA BE...
THE TOP STAR OF THE TROUPE!
THAT'S RIGHT!!
THAT'S WHERE I'M HEADED!
I'LL GO STRAIGHT TO THE TOP!!

TODAY, WATANABE SARASA...

MADE LOTS OF ENEMIES.

THERE ARE EIGHTY MEMBERS IN EACH TROUPE.

BETWEEN SPRING, SUMMER, AUTUMN, AND WINTER, THERE ARE 320 MEMBERS.

THAT MEANS OUT OF ALL OF THEM...

ONLY **FOUR** GET TO BE THE TOP STARS.

YOU'RE A COCKY ONE, HUH?

WHY DO YOU SAY THAT?

WHAT AN AIRHEAD.

WHAT THE HELL WAS THAT POSE WATANABE JUST DID?
KICK-BOXING?
CAPOEI-RA?
SOME KIND OF MARTIAL ART.
IT WAS A FUMIDASHI STAMP.

HUH?!
KIRISHIMA-SENSEI!? YOU MEAN LIKE IN SUMO?!
OH!
NO, NOT SUMO.
?
HER FUMIDASHI REMINDED ME OF THE ONE FROM SUKEROKU.
THE KABUKI PLAY.
SOME WONDERED WHAT THE TEACHERS WERE EXPECTING FROM WATANABE SARASA.
OTHERS WONDERED WHO'D BE THE TOP STAR OF OUR CLASS.
AI-CHAN!
LET'S WALK HOME TOGETHER!
I DIDN'T CARE ABOUT EITHER OF THOSE THINGS.
TMP TMP TMP TMP

DOES EVERYONE HAVE A COPY OF THE ROSTER?
HERE ARE THE GIRLS WE'RE KEEPING OUR EYES ON. NARATA AI, OF COURSE.
HOSHI-NO KAORU.
WATA-NABE SARASA.
WHO'S HOSH-NO?
HER MOTHER AND GRANDMA WERE IN THE KOUKA TROUPE.
A LEGACY KID, EH?
SHE TRIED TO GET IN AND FAILED TWICE, RIGHT?
WATA-NABE?
THE TALL CHICK?
OH, LITTLE MISS OSCAR.
HOW COCKY CAN YOU GET?
COCKY? MORE LIKE DUMB!
RIGHT.
WHO'S TAKING WHO?

4

AI-CHAN, LOOK! TA-DA!
IT'S THE KOUKA UNIFORM!
くる SPIN
くる SPIN
I KNOW.
I'VE GOT ONE, TOO.
WE WORE IT YESTER-DAY.
GUIDANCE WEEK IS OVER, AND WE HAD OUR ENTRANCE CEREMONY, TOO.
TOMOR-ROW, WE FINALLY START CLASSES FOR REAL!
I'M SO HYPED!!

SO SHE SAID, BUT THIS MORNING...
THIS TIME...
I'LL AT LEAST TRY AND WAKE HER UP.
WAKE UP.
C'MON.
......
TUNK
TOSS
NOT MY FAULT SHE DIDN'T GET UP.

MORNING, NARATA-SAN.

HI, SUGIMOTO-SAN.

WHERE'S WATANABE-SAN?

I TRIED WAKING HER UP, BUT NO DICE.

!!

THAT'S NOT GOOD!

SORRY, I NEED TO GET IN YOUR ROOM!

FINE.

WATANABE-SAN!

WATA-NABE-SAN!!

ZZZ!

WATANABE SARASA...!

GET THE HELL UP!!
WAUGH!
WHY'S SUGIMOTO-SAN SO BOSSY?
SHE'S THE FRESHMAN REP 'CAUSE SHE GOT THE TOP SCORE ON THE ENTRANCE EXAM.
!!
THAT'S SUPER COOL!

HURRY INTO THE AUDITORI-UM!
BUT NO RUNNING!
AUDITORIUM? ARE THOSE MILITARY GUYS HERE AGAIN?
NO, SOMEONE FAR SCARIER.
DON'T SAY A WORD FROM HERE ON OUT!
LET'S GO!
GOOD MORNING!
PLEASE FORGIVE US FOR BEING LATE. THIRTY-NINE OF THE FORTY NEW STUDENTS ARE HERE!
IT'S OKAY, YOU'RE NOT LATE.
IT'S ONLY FIVE MINUTES TO SIX.
WELCOME, NEW STUDENTS.
I'M TAKEI, THE UPPER-CLASSMAN REPRESEN-TATIVE.
BEFORE YOU BEGIN YOUR FIRST REAL DAY OF CLASS...

WE'RE HERE TO TEACH YOU ONE OF THE SCHOOL'S TRADI-TIONS!
MORNING CLEANING.

EACH NEW STUDENT WILL BE PAIRED WITH AN UPPER-CLASSMAN.
PLEASE FIND YOUR UPPERCLASS-MAN WHEN YOUR NAME IS CALLED.

THIS UPPER-CLASSMAN WILL ALSO BE PROVIDING YOU WITH ADVICE AND GUIDANCE THROUGH THE YEAR.
SO GET TO KNOW THEM WELL.

!!
Like a big sister!!
LIKE IN A SORORITY!
Really? That's so lame.
This is just like another manga by *RoV*'s Riyoko Ikeda, *Dear Brother*!
That's about her "brother" though, not a sorority sister.
?
Or maybe it'll be like *Maria Watches Over Us*!
DON'T LOOK AT ME!
I have no idea, but it's not gonna be as pretty or nice.

Depending on who you get, your next year might be a living hell.
ICHI-KAWA-SAN.
HERE!
LOUD-ER!
HERE!
NARATA-SAN.
HERE.

I'M NOJIMA HIJIRI, VICE PRINCIPAL OF THE STUDENT COUNCIL.
NICE TO MEET YOU!
NICE TO MEET YOU, TOO.

AWWW! AI-CHAN'S BIG SIS LOOKS SO SWEET!
WATA-NABE-SAN.

WATANABE SARASA!!
AH!
PRESENT!
FWISH
COME WHEN YOU'RE CALLED!
VA-VOOM!
TIGHT
HIP-HIP-HOORAY!
I'M NAKAYAMA RISA.
I'LL BE IN CHARGE OF YOU FOR THE NEXT YEAR.

OH MY GOSH! MY BIG SISTER'S A SUPER-HOT GIRL WITH A COOL ATTITUDE! ♡
IS SHE GOING TO BE OKAY?
YOU'RE GOING TO CLEAN THIS DANCE STUDIO FROM TOP TO BOTTOM IN THE NEXT TWO HOURS.
TWO HOURS ?!
SOME-THING WRONG?
NOPE! I'M ON IT!
LAST YEAR, THIS WAS MY CLASS-ROOM TO CLEAN.
BUT THERE'LL BE TWO PEOPLE DOING THIS ROOM, SO YOU'LL TAKE THIS HALF.
ONCE YOU'RE DONE WIPING THE FLOORS, YOU'LL USE THESE HAIRPINS AND BRUSHES TO CLEAN OUT THE DIRT FROM THE CORNERS AND CREVICES.
THEN, YOU'LL WIPE THE DUST FROM THE WINDOWS AND MIRROR. IT NEEDS TO PASS THE WHITE GLOVE INSPECTION!
WE CLEAN THE SCHOOL FROM TOP TO BOTTOM EVERY DAY!
OH, THERE'S OUR SECOND PERSON.

HUH? WHERE'S YOUR FRESHMAN?
SHE'S NOT HERE TODAY. THERE WAS SOME KIND OF FAMILY EMERGENCY.
HUNH.
THAT'S OKAY! I CAN DO IT!
REALLY?! THANKS!
I NEED TO PRACTICE THE HOME-WORK FOR PIANO CLASS...
SO, I'LL BE IN THE PIANO PRAC-TICE ROOM!
TURN
RIGHT THEN, START WITH THE FLOOR.
OKAY!
AND DO IT RIGHT, OR YOU'LL BE HERE ALL DAY!
OKAY!

HEY, HOW TALL ARE YOU?
I'M 178 CM!
WOW.
AND HOW OLD ARE YOU?
FIF-TEEN! ♡
HUNH. SO, YOU'RE STRAIGHT OUT OF MIDDLE SCHOOL.
YEAH, BUT NOW I'M TOO OLD TO PILOT AN EVA.
WHAT? ARE YOU AN IDIOT?
YOU SOUND JUST LIKE ASUKA!!
CAN YOU NOT?
JEEZ! YOU'RE AS AN-NOYING AS THE RUMORS SAY.
I GOT IN HERE WHEN I WAS A SENIOR IN HIGH SCHOOL, SO I'M NINETEEN.
I'LL BE TWENTY NEXT YEAR.

SO.
YOU WANT TO BE OSCAR?
YUP! THAT'S WHY I'M HERE!
TO BE THE BEST OSCAR!
WELL, YOU WON'T.
SOME-ONE LIKE YOU COULD NEVER BE OSCAR.
SORRY!

WHAAA ...?
WH-WHY ?!
TATAMI ROOM
START BY SWEEPING THE ROOM.
HUH? HEY!
SHWOO
WHY'D YOU START IN THE MIDDLE?
YOU HAVE TO START AT ONE END!
SORRY.
I'VE NEVER CLEANED A ROOM LIKE THIS BEFORE.
OH... I MEAN, I'M NOT SURPRISED.
BUT THIS ROOM IS YOUR RESPONSIBILITY NOW!
START IN ONE OF THE CORNERS, OKAY? LIKE OVER HERE.

WOW, NARATA-SAN!

YOU HAVE SUCH LONG EYE-LASHES.

AND YOUR SKIN IS SO CLEAR!

......

NO WONDER YOU GOT TO BE IN JPX! ♡

THANKS.
YOU KNOW, EVERYONE WAS FIGHTING OVER WHO GOT TO BE YOUR BIG SISTER.

WE HAD A BIG ROCK-PAPER-SCISSORS TOURNAMENT FOR IT! ♡
I FEEL LIKE I'VE BEEN PULLED UP ON STAGE FOR A JPX NUMBER!
TEE HEE!

I SEE.

SO, UH...
I'M ACTUALLY A HUGE FAN OF JPX48.
IF I HADN'T GOTTEN INTO KOUKA, I WAS GOING TO AUDITION FOR THEM.

EVERYONE IN JPX48 IS SO ENERGETIC, WITH THOSE BIG SMILES AND TWINKLING EYES. THEY'RE ALL SO CUTE!
BUT IF I'M NOT IN THE GROUP, AT LEAST I GET TO BE YOUR STUDENT ADVISOR.
UH-HUH.

SO, I'M GUESSING...
YOU WEREN'T A BIG FAN OF MINE, THEN?

WHY DO YOU SAY THAT?

BECAUSE I'M NOT ENERGETIC, AND I DON'T HAVE A BIG SMILE, OR TWINKLING EYES.

BUT I LIKED YOU TOO, NARATA-SAN! YOU WERE, LIKE, THE COOL BEAUTY OF THE GROUP!

IT'S FINE.

WELL... I WAS A REALLY BIG FAN OF MOMO-CHAN.

OH, YEAH. SHE WAS ALWAYS GO, GO, GO.

I DON'T CARE.

......

UH.

NEXT, YOU'LL CLEAN THE TATAMI. GO FILL THE BUCKET WITH WATER AND GET A RAG WET.

OKAY.

UM?

NARATA-SAN?

I'M LOOKING FORWARD TO HELPING YOU THIS YEAR. ♡

AND I THINK YOU'RE GOING TO BE GLAD YOU HAVE ME.

THERE ARE LOTS OF UPPER-CLASSMEN WHO AREN'T THAT NICE TO THEIR FRESHMEN.

WH-WH-WHUUUU...?

WHU-WHY CAN'D I BE OSGAR?!

OH MY GOD, QUIT CRYING!
STOP IT, YOU BABY!
YOU'RE MAKING ME FEEL LIKE A BIG BULLY!
BUH...
B-BUH...

I HAVEN'T EVEN GOTTEN TO TAKE CLASSES YET!

HOW DO YOU KNOW I CAN'T BE OSCAR?

LOOK, I'M SORRY! I LIED, YOU CAN TOTALLY DO IT.
YOU'RE LYING NOW! TELL ME *WHY*!

HER HEIGHT...
SHE'S WAY TOO TALL TO BE OSCAR.
UNLESS THERE'S ANOTHER GIRL WHO'S TALLER THAN HER THAT CAN BE ANDRÉ.
THAT, AND...
NOBODY WANTED TO BE YOUR STUDENT ADVISOR...
AND STANDING OUT IN A GROUP OF GIRLS IS BASICALLY SIGNING YOUR OWN DEATH WARRANT.

BUT IF SHE WERE TO UNDERSTAND THE REALITY OF HER SITUATION...

WHAT WOULD HAPPEN TO HER?

Wow, you wanna be the top musume-yaku too, Risa?

I mean, you *are* really pretty.

You might be better than everyone else in the group...

but your voice, face... basically, *everything*... it just doesn't suit the role of a young woman.

You'd be way better off playing the roles for older women as an onnayaku.
Like Jeanne, or Carlotta, or Kurotokage! Those roles would be **perfect** for you! Everyone says so!

Too bad you're not taller!
You could've been a top otokoyaku!

SOB!
SOB!
SOB!
I'LL GIVE HER ONE THING.
SHE'S ABLE TO CLEAN AND CRY. AND SHE'S ACTUALLY DOING A GOOD JOB.
STILL HARD TO WATCH.
UHH? HEY.
I HEARD YOU STOOD UNDER THE CHERRY TREE BEFORE YOU WERE ADMITTED, RIGHT?
DIDN'T YOU HEAR THE URBAN LEGEND? IT'S BAD LUCK!
IF YOU STAND THERE BEFORE BEING ADMITTED, YOU'LL NEVER BE THE TOP ACTRESS!
THAT LEGEND'S HELD TRUE FOR A HUNDRED YEARS!

IS THAT TRUE?
YUP!
FINE, THEN!
I'LL BE THE ONE TO BREAK THE CURSE!

MAYBE I COULDN'T IF I WERE A GUY...
BUT I WAS LUCKY ENOUGH TO BE BORN A GIRL!
AND LUCKY ENOUGH TO GET INTO THIS SCHOOL!
YOU NEVER KNOW WHAT SOMEONE MIGHT ACCOMPLISH!
GRIP
THAT'S WHY I'M GOING TO DO IT!
I'M GOING TO SHOW YOU THAT MYTH IS TOTALLY FAKE!

BACK THEN ...
I THOUGHT A GIRL LIKE HIJIRI, WITH HER ANGELIC SMILE AND UNSHAKE-ABLE CONFI-DENCE...

WOULD BE THE TOP MUSUME-YAKU FOR SURE.

IT TAKES MORE THAN DREAMS AND WISHES TO SUCCEED AT KOUKA.
BUT...

I'LL USE MAHOTAN FROM DQ TO REFLECT THIS CURSE AWAY FROM ME!
......

ARE GAMES AND ANIME ALL YOU THINK ABOUT?

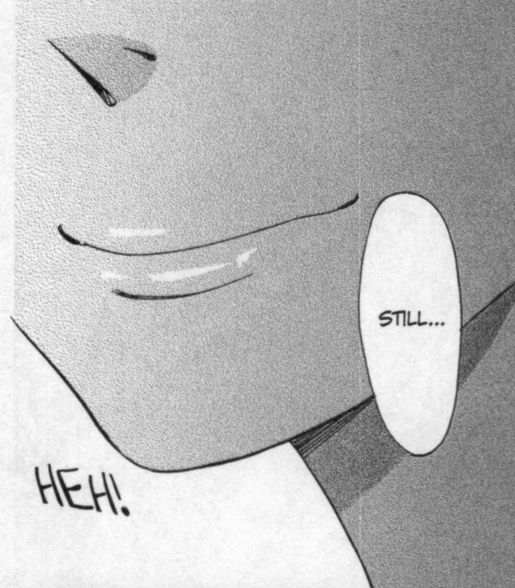
STILL...
HEH!

YOU'RE RIGHT. NOBODY KNOWS WHAT THE FUTURE HOLDS.
TRY YOUR BEST, YEAH?
I WILL!
I WILL, TOO.
OH, CRAP. IT'S ALMOST TIME FOR FIRST PERIOD.
WHO DO YOU HAVE FIRST?
ACTING WITH ANDOU-SENSEI!
OH, THE PHANTOM, HUH? THEN YOU DON'T NEED TIME TO CHANGE.
PHANTOM?
SO, YOU'LL CLEAN THE ROOM UNTIL IT'S TIME TO GO!
I'LL HELP OUT, TOO.
HUH? BUT...
IT'S FINE! JUST THIS ONCE, GOT IT?
PLUS, I WASTED A BUNCH OF TIME TALKING.
C'MON, LET'S GET TO WORK!
BA-DMP! ♡
BIG SISTER! ♡

HEE HEE! HI, Y'ALL! ♡
HERE'S A MILITARY SALUTE FOR YA! ♡

カ KA-
OH.
チャ CHAK

PHEW! WE WERE WORRIED ABOUT YOU.
WORRIED THE UPPER-YEARS HAD DONE YOU IN.
I HEARD YOUR STUDENT ADVISOR IS A REAL HARD-ASS!
WHAT'S SHE LIKE, WATANABE-SAN?

SHE'S JUST A STRAIGHT SHOOTER!
SHE WAS REALLY NICE!
OH? BORING!
OUR SENPAI WAS SO SCARY!
I DROPPED THE BROOM, AND SHE STARED AT ME LIKE SHE WAS GONNA MURDER ME!
YOUR ADVISOR SEEMS REALLY SWEET, NARATA-SAN.

......
CLAK...
YOU THINK SO?
OH MY GOSH!
NARACCHI WAS SOOOO CUTE, LIKE A LITTLE DOLL!
NO WONDER SHE WAS IN JPX48! ♡
HA HA!
OH, RISA.
HOW WAS LITTLE MISS OSCAR?
FINE. SHE'S JUST A KID WHO LOVES ANIME AND VIDEO GAMES.
HIJIRI'S THE ONE WHO NEEDS TO BE WORRIED.
PEOPLE ARE SAYING THAT NARACCHI COULD BE THE NEXT TOP MUSUMEYAKU. YOU BETTER LOOK OUT!

I'M NOT SURE WHAT YOU'RE IMPLYING.
BUT NO NEED TO WORRY ABOUT *ME!*
NARACCHI IS CUTE BUT SHE DOESN'T HAVE THE DRIVE.
I GUESS WE'LL SEE.
NOBODY CAN PREDICT THE FUTURE, AFTER ALL!

Chapter 5
Don't be ridiculous!
MII
MIN
I don't care how good your chances are!
Or how talented you may be!
MIIN
It's simply impossible!
No matter how hard you try...

*Sukeroku is a role in a kabuki play, and only men can perform kabuki.

MIN
MIN
SHAAAAA
RUMBLE
WAS THAT THUNDER?
UGH! I HOPE NOT!
MORNING, NARATA-SAN!
MORNING.
WHERE'S WATANABE-SAN? IS SHE AWAKE?
NO IDEA.
SPLASH
LOYAL BLUE
5
CAMPUS

THAT'S NOT GOOD! IF SHE'S LATE, WE ALL GET IN TROUBLE!
IF EVEN ONE OF US MESSES UP, WE ALL GET LECTURED ABOUT IT.
WE COULD BE USING THAT TIME TO PRACTICE INSTEAD.
I KNOW I MIGHT BE OUT OF LINE ASKING THIS...
BUT WOULD IT KILL YOU TO TAKE MORE OF AN INTEREST IN OTHER PEOPLE?
AN INTEREST IN OTHERS?

ARE OTHER PEOPLE ALWAYS ...
GETTING UP IN EACH OTHER'S BUSINESS?
WATANABE-SAN?
YOU AWAKE?
FLASH
RUMMBLE
OH... GOOD MORNING...
AI-CHAN.

GOOD MORNING.
OH, ANDOU-SENSEI, YOU'RE IN EARLY.
I DIDN'T WANNA SLIP AND GET HURT ON THE TRAIN PLATFORM.
IT GETS DANGEROUS WHEN IT'S RUSH HOUR.
I WOULD'VE GIVEN YOU A RIDE.
I'D LOVE TO HELP TOO! ♡
NO THANKS.
CAN'T BELIEVE IT'S GONNA RAIN ALL DAY.
Osaka
Nagoya
Kochi
PWP
Kabuki Actor: Shirakawa Kaou
THE ART OF KABUKI HAS BEEN PRESERVED AND PASSED DOWN SINCE ITS INCEPTION 400 YEARS AGO, AND THE MISATOYA TROUPE EMBODIES ITS STYLE AND GRACE.
ENTER THE MAN WHO CRITICS CALL A NATIONAL TREASURE, KAOU.
OH.
KAOU'S NHK DOCUMENTARY'S ON TONIGHT. GOTTA WATCH IT.
I'M GONNA WATCH IT!

HMMM.
I HAVE NO DIRECT DESCENDANT TO TAKE ON MY POSITION.
EVEN NOW, I'M UNSURE OF WHAT TO DO.
CONGRATS
PERHAPS SOMEONE NOT OF MY BLOOD WILL INHERIT IT INSTEAD.
HUH?
WHAT ABOUT KOUZABURO, THE GUY NEXT TO HIM? ISN'T THAT HIS SON?
SON-IN-LAW. HE'S POPULAR AND HAS THE SKILLS.
BUT SINCE THEY'RE NOT RELATED BY BLOOD, HE TECHNICALLY CAN'T BECOME THE 16TH KAOU.
RUB
AND SINCE HE AND HIS WIFE DON'T HAVE ANY SONS, WELL...
HUNH. AND I'M GUESSING THEY WON'T BREAK TRADITION AND HAVE A STUDENT TAKE OVER INSTEAD.
WATCH THE REST TONIGHT AT NINE P.M.
OOH!
I SAW SHIRAKAWA AKIYA ON-SCREEN FOR A SECOND! ♡
HE'S SEVENTEEN, RIGHT? HE'S A CUTE KID.
YOU GUYS SURE ARE HAVING FUN.
HEY, YOU HANDLED CLASS A'S FIRST ACTUAL CLASS, RIGHT?
DID YOU MAKE THEM DO INTRODUCTIONS?
NOPE. WHY?
I THOUGHT SO! CLASS A SEEMED OFF FOR SOME REASON.
THEY WERE ALL SO COLD AND UPTIGHT!
I HAD CLASS B'S FIRST CLASS!

THEY'RE ONLY SPLIT INTO THESE GROUPS FOR CLASS, THOUGH, RIGHT?
NARATA-SENSEI'S RIGHT! CLASS A IS ON EDGE!
IT'S A GROUP OF TEENAGE GIRLS! OF COURSE THEY'RE ALL ON EDGE!
MY WORD! I NEVER EXPECTED SUCH SEXISM FROM YOU!
JAB
MAKE THEM DO INTRODUCTIONS!!
RUMBLE...
SO, BECAUSE NARATA-SENSEI WON'T SHUT UP ABOUT IT...
WE'RE ALL GOING TO INTRODUCE OURSELVES.

THANKS A LOT, TAICHI.
SENSEI!

WEREN'T WE GOING TO STUDY SHAKE-SPEARE TODAY?

I DON'T WANT TO MISS OUT ON ACTUAL LESSONS!
SAME!
ME TOO!

SEE? EVERY-ONE IS THE SAME AS ME.

I CAME HERE TO WORK HARD AND LEARN!

YEAH.
I FIGURED.

THERE'S NO POINT IN INTRO-DUCING OURSELVES NOW!

THEY'RE ALL FOCUSED ON THEM-SELVES.

NOBODY HERE IS INTERESTED IN ANYONE ELSE.

WELL, EXCEPT ...

FOR HER.
RATTLE
RATTLE
GLINT
GLINT
...
OKAY, LISTEN!
I KNOW THIS ISN'T A NORMAL SCHOOL.
BELIEVE ME, I KNOW.

IN A NORMAL SCHOOL, YOU'D GET THREE YEARS TOGETHER.
AND YOU SURE AS HELL WOULDN'T KNOW FOR SURE WHAT YOU WANTED TO DO IN THE FUTURE.
YOU COULD GO ON TO COLLEGE, FIND A JOB, OR TAKE WHATEVER CAREER PATH YOU WANTED.

HERE, THOUGH...
YOU'VE GOT TWO PATHS TO PICK FROM.

SINK OR SWIM.

KEEP GOING... OR QUIT.

WHEN YOU GRADUATE FROM HERE...
YOU'LL JOIN THE KOUKA TROUPE.
THAT WILL BE YOUR JOB.

SO, UNTIL YOU DECIDE TO QUIT...
YOU'RE STUCK TOGETHER! ☆
GRIN

SO, YOU REALLY NEED TO LEARN ABOUT EACH OTHER...
BECAUSE YOU'RE GOING TO BE LIVING SIDE-BY-SIDE FOR A *LOOONG* TIME.

ALL RIGHT, SENSEI!
ガタ
CLATTER
ALLOW ME TO GET THE BALL ROLLING.
OH, LITTLE MISS PERFECT!
THE GIRLS WHO GET INTO THIS SCHOOL...
I'M SUGIMOTO SAWA, FIRST-YEAR CLASS REPRESENTATIVE. I'M SIXTEEN YEARS OLD.
MY FAMILY RUNS A BALLET STUDIO UP IN TOKYO.
I'VE BEEN DOING BALLET MY WHOLE LIFE.
DIDN'T GET IN BECAUSE THEIR PARENTS OR RECRUITERS WERE PUSHING FOR THEIR ADMISSION.
I CONSIDERED STUDYING BALLET IN PARIS, BUT MY TRUE LOVE IS MUSICAL THEATER.
THAT'S WHY I CAME TO THE KOUKA SCHOOL OF MUSICAL AND THEATRICAL ARTS.
I'M GLAD TO BE HERE WITH YOU ALL.
THEY GOT IN BECAUSE THEY REALLY WANTED TO BE HERE.
I WON THE MISS SNOW CRAB BEAUTY PAGEANT IN MY HOME CITY!
I PERFORMED IN THE KOMAWARI ACTING TROUPE WHEN I WAS LITTLE!
THEY BROKE DOWN THE DOOR THROUGH SHEER FORCE OF WILL.
MY FATHER IS A PROFESSOR AT A MUSIC CONSERVATORY!

I'M HOSHINO KAORU, AND I'M EIGHTEEN.
MY MOTHER IS SHIRAKAZE MIYUKI, FORMER MUSUME-YAKU IN THE SPRING TROUPE.
THEY'RE CONFIDENT IN THEIR ABILITIES.
MY GRAND-MOTHER WAS A MUSUME-YAKU IN THE SPRING TROUPE, TOO.
I'M THE THIRD GENERATION OF GIRLS IN MY FAMILY TO JOIN THE KOUKA TROUPE!!
BUT BECAUSE I WAS BLESSED WITH SUCH INCREDIBLE HEIGHT...
I WANT TO PLAY MALE ROLES AS AN OTOKO-YAKU!!
THEY'RE FEARLESS FIGHTERS.
I'M SAWADA CHIAKI!
AND I'M SAWADA CHIKA!
WE GREW UP WATCHING THE KOUKA TROUPE PERFORM!
LAST YEAR, CHIKA GOT IN, BUT I DIDN'T.
SO, WE TRIED AGAIN THIS YEAR AND BOTH GOT IN!
THAT MEANS THE WEAK WILL QUICKLY BE WEEDED OUT.

UMM! I'M YAMADA AYAKO.
I'VE ALWAYS DREAMED OF JOINING THE KOUKA TROUPE. I NEVER THOUGHT I'D ACTUALLY GET IN...
B-BUT I'M GOING TO GIVE IT MY ALL!
THAT GIRL'S IN FOR A ROUGH TIME.

I GUESS I'M THE ONLY ONE HERE WHO DOESN'T REALLY CARE ABOUT KOUKA ITSELF.
ガタッ
CLATTER

I'M WATANABE SARASA, AND I'M FIFTEEN! ☆
I REALLY LOVE LADY OSCAR...
WE KNOW.
YOU TOLD US ALREADY!
YOU WANNA BE THE TOP STAR, RIGHT?
YES! BEFORE LUFFY BECOMES THE PIRATE KING, IF I CAN!
SO, UH...

Sign: Watanabe Tatami

I LOVE ANIME, MANGA, AND HISTORICAL TV SHOWS.
I LIVE IN A SMALL SUBURB OF TOKYO...
WITH MY GRANDPA, WHO OWNS A TATAMI SHOP.
SHAKE
SHAKE
JUST THE TWO OF YOU?
YUP!
OH, AND MY CAT NONO-CHAN!

BUT NONO-CHAN DOESN'T REALLY LIKE PEOPLE!
BLAH
HER NOSE IS ALWAYS SNIFFING AT US LIKE SHE DOESN'T TRUST US, AND...
BLAH
BLAH
I'M SURE NONO-CHAN'S GREAT.
BUT I HAVE TO STOP YOU THERE.
WE NEED TO MOVE ON.

OKAY, LAST ONE, YOU'RE UP.
MURMUR

I'M NARATA AI. I'M SIXTEEN.
I DID BALLET WHEN I WAS LITTLE.
MY BALLET TEACHER WAS MY GRANDFATHER...
THE FAMOUS NARATA TAICHI.
WHOA!
I DIDN'T KNOW THAT!
I LEARNED A BIT OF SINGING AND DANCING, TOO.
THAT'S IT.
THAT'S IT?
THERE'S GOTTA BE MORE!
......

MY MOTHER'S THE ACTRESS NARATA KIMIKO.
I WAS IN JPX48 UNTIL I QUIT...
NO, UNTIL THEY MADE ME QUIT.
THAT'S ALL.
キ BING ーン
コ BONG ーン
どばざー
BA-SHAAA
カ BENG ーン
STOP.
OH, THAT'S THE BELL.
AH, RIGHT.
コ BOONG ーン
JUST STOP.
STOP LOOKING AT ME LIKE THAT.
DON'T GO SHARING ALL THIS ON SNAPCHAT OR WHAT-EVER. YOU COULD GET EXPELLED.
GOT IT?

OH MY GOD, YOU WERE IN JPX, AI-CHAN?!
JUST STOP!
ひゃあああ
EEEEK!
First-Years
I HAD NO IDEA!
OH, WOW! ♡
YOU'RE SO CUTE! ♡
I COULD JUST EAT YOU UP!
OH, MAN! I WANT TO WEAR SOMETHING AS CUTE AS THIS SOMEDAY!
HEY, WATANABE-SAN, DO YOU ALWAYS CARRY THAT TABLET AROUND WITH YOU?
HEE HEE! I GOT IT AS A PRESENT FOR GETTING INTO KOUKA!
REALLY? THAT'S NICE.
BUT YOU HEARD ANDOU-SENSEI, RIGHT?

YOU'RE NOT GOING TO POST THINGS ON YOUR BLOG OR TWITTER, ARE YOU?
DON'T WORRY!
I HAVE TWITTER, BUT I'VE ONLY GOT TWO FOLLOWERS.

WAIT, TWO? I THOUGHT YOU ONLY LIVED WITH YOUR GRANDPA.
IS YOUR CAT FOLLOWING YOU, TOO?

OH MY GOSH, OF COURSE NOT! YOU ARE SOOO FUNNY, SUGIMOTO-SAN!
YEAH, SURE.
TWITCH
TWITCH

MY TWO FOLLOWERS ARE MY GRANDPA AND MY BOYFRIEND.
TEXTING'S NICE AND ALL, BUT I ALWAYS FEEL LIKE I HAVE TO RESPOND RIGHT AWAY.
WITH TWITTER, I CAN JUST POST AND REPLY WHENEVER I WANT. SO I USE THAT TO TALK ABOUT WHAT I'M DOING EVERY DAY! ♡

HUNH. THAT MAKES SENSE.

WAIT, BOY-FRIEND ...?

GASP
NOM
WHAT DID SHE JUST SAY???!!
SHAAAA
I DON'T GET IT!

DO YOU THINK SHE ACTUALLY *HAS* A BOYFRIEND?
IF SHE DOES, HE'S GOT INTERESTING TASTE.
WELL, THEY SAY THERE'S SOMEONE FOR EVERYONE.
MAYBE SHE'S JUST PRETENDING.
DOES ANYONE HERE HAVE A BOYFRIEND?

WE DON'T! NEVER HAD ONE, EITHER!
WHAT'S WRONG WITH THAT?
S-SAME HERE.
GLAD IT'S NOT JUST ME!
I BROKE UP WITH HIM BEFORE I STARTED HERE!
YEAH, SAME.

WHERE *IS* WATANABE-SAN?
SHE LEFT BEFORE WE GOT IN.
WHY IS EVERYONE TALKING ABOUT WATANABE SARASA?

THEY'VE ALWAYS GOT THEIR EYES ON HER.
THE SHIRA-KAWA KAOU DOCUMEN-TARY.
OH.

BOW
ペコッ
THANK YOU FOR LETTING US USE THE BATHS.

UH...

ALL GOOD. YOU CAN COME WATCH IF YOU WANT.
YOU MIGHT LEARN SOMETHING.

ONE OF YOUR CLASSMATES IS ALREADY HERE.

THERE'S A SEAT OPEN IN THE FRONT, NARATA-SAN. FEEL FREE TO TAKE IT.

THANKS BUT NO THANKS.

INHERITING A POSITION...
DOESN'T MEAN YOU NEED TO TAKE ON THE NAME ITSELF.
IT'S REALLY ABOUT...
INHERITING THE SOUL!

THE HEART AND SOUL OF THIS COMPANY HAS BEEN PASSED DOWN SINCE THE EDO PERIOD!
THE INHERI-TANCE SYSTEM IS SO WEIRD.
LOYAL BLUE

IS KAOU-SAN SCARY? YOU BET HE IS!
IF I MESS UP EVEN A LITTLE, HE STARTS SHOUTING AT ME HOW I'M "THE WORST" AND HOW I SHOULD "JUST QUIT."
OH, THAT'S SHIRA-KAWA KOUZA-BUROU!
GOD, HE'S SEXY.
SHION REI FROM THE AUTUMN TROUPE IS WAY SEXIER THAN HIM, THOUGH.

OF COURSE SHE IS!

EXCUSE ME, GIRLS, BUT IS WATA-NABE-SAN HERE?
QUIET IN THE HALL

YEP, RIGHT HERE!
OH, THANK GOOD-NESS!
I'M ABOUT TO LEAVE, BUT SOME PACKAGES ARRIVED FOR YOU. I BELIEVE THEY'RE FROM HOME?
OH, THEY'RE FROM MY GRANDPA!
HEE HEE! I WONDER WHAT'S INSIDE?

NOW'S OUR CHANCE!
SNATCH
!!
Hurry! It's not locked, you can get in!
Open Twitter! Quick!!
I'm going for it!
JiraiyaBot @Jira
Morning!
Sarasa @Sara3
Morning! Boy, did you hear the thunder?
GranpaKen
@sara3 I like a nice, traditional Japanese meal for breakfast.
JIRAIYA-BOT?
A BOT?!!

WHAT THE HECK?
IS THAT SOME ANIME CHARAC-TER?
SHE'S SUCH AN OTAKU.
IS THAT IT?!
PUT IT BACK WHERE SHE LEFT IT.
OWWW...

"WOULD IT KILL YOU TO TAKE MORE OF AN INTEREST IN OTHER PEOPLE?"

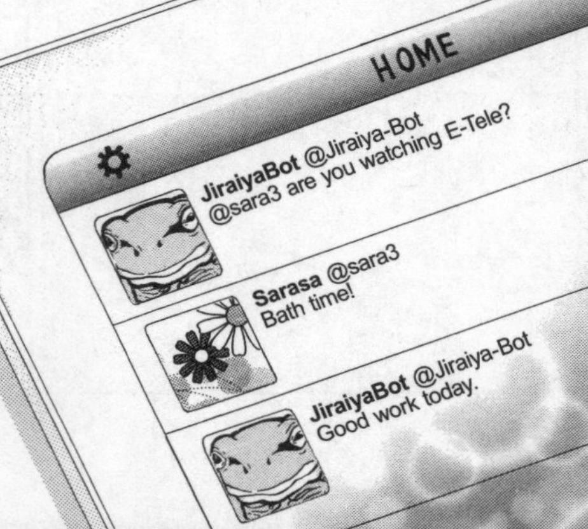

@sara3 are you watching E-Tele?

Bath time!

Good work today.

OH, THAT'S SHIRAKAWA AKIYA.
HE'S PRETTY POPULAR WITH THE OLDER LADIES. PROBABLY BECAUSE HE'S SO CUTE!
BUT OTOKOYAKU AOI TSUKIYA IN THE SUMMER TROUPE IS WAY CUTER.
OF COURSE SHE IS!
HUH?
HUH? WHICH ROLE WOULD I LIKE TO PLAY?
BOY, THAT'S TOUGH. I DON'T WANT TO MAKE MY MASTER MAD OR ANYTHING.
JiraiyaBot @Jiraiya-Bot
I'm on TV right now (^_^)
HMM.
YOU KNOW WHAT, I'LL MAKE HIM A LITTLE MAD.

I WANT TO PLAY...
JiraiyaBot @Jiraiya-Bot
@Sara3 He totally got mad at me after that lmao
SUKE-ROKU.
WOW! HE SENT ME A BUNCH OF RAI-OKOSHI RICE SNACKS! PLEASE HAVE SOME, MA'AM! ♡
RAI-OKOSHI
OH, THANK YOU! ♥

6

HOME
Search
Jump Magazine's Noraemon
OT!
Sarasa @Sara3
First period's ballet today!
I feel so girly wearing my leotard
Everyone in my class is so good
Jiraiyabot @Jiraiya-Bot
@sara3 Morning!
I've got practice today.

SHFF

WHAT'S UP, KOUZABUROU?
YOU'RE ON TWITTER, RIGHT? LET ME SEE.
WHAT?! NO!
TUG TUG
I JUST WANT TO CHECK THAT YOU AND SARASA-SAN ARE KEEPING IT CLEAN.
NOBODY ASKED YOU TO CHECK!
AKIYA...
WHO BOUGHT YOU THAT IPAD?

OOOH! SARASA-SAN HAS BALLET THIS MORNING?

MAYBE I SHOULD SEND HER A SIGNED TUTU.
KOUKA'S NOT A BALLET SCHOOL, YOU KNOW.

ALSO, A SIGNED TUTU? THAT'S WEIRD.
AKIYA.
I WANT TO BE HER SECRET SUPPORTER, LIKE THE PURPLE ROSE.
FROM GLASS MASK*?
THAT'S RIGHT!

*Glass Mask *is a shojo series about an aspiring actress.*

SHE'S FIFTEEN? BOY, SHE'S GROWN SO MUCH!
YOU CAN SAY THAT AGAIN.
SHE'S TALLER THAN I AM!

HMM.
SHE WAS SHORTER WHEN WE WERE TRAINING TOGETHER WAY BACK WHEN.
EVERY TIME I SAW HER, SHE'D FOLLOW ME AROUND LIKE A CUTE LITTLE PUPPY!
I WISH I HAD A GIRL LIKE HER.
BUT SHE'S DOWN IN KOBE NOW, HUH?
CANCEL
@sara3 Good luck at ballet practice!
QWER
ASDFG

MAYBE I SHOULD GO VISIT.
WAY TO BE A STALKER.
GENTLY, NOW.
FOLLOW THE MUSIC.

PASSE.
STRETCH YOUR LEG OUT FROM THE CENTER...
AND ARA-BESQUE.
HOLD IT THERE.
SEE HOW LONG YOU CAN HOLD IT.
WELL DONE, SUGIMOTO-SAN.
NARATA-SAN, OPEN YOUR SHOULDERS MORE.

WATANABE-SAN...
YOU LOOK MORE LIKE SHIMURA THAN ANY-THING.
PFFT!
SHIMURA FROM GIN TAMA?!
NO, SHIMURA KEN, THE COMEDIAN.
DON'T FLEX YOUR FINGERS LIKE THAT.
AND TRY TO LIFT YOUR LEG A LITTLE MORE.
THIS IS AS HIGH AS IT GOES!
THINK OF IT AS STRETCHING OUT.
IT... IT'S HARD!
DON'T CLENCH YOUR BUTT.

STILL, SHE'S HELD THAT POSE FOR FIFTEEN SECONDS.
OKAY, YOU CAN RELAX.
YOU'VE GOT A BAD HABIT WHERE YOU STAMP YOUR FEET TOO HARD DURING BARRE EXERCISES.
WHERE'D THAT COME FROM?
!!
MY OLD TEACHER TOLD ME THE SAME THING!
OH, YEAH? WHAT ACADEMY DID YOU GO TO?
THE BIG OUTDOORS ACADEMY!
THAT'S A WEIRD NAME.
WHERE WAS IT?
ASAKUSA, TOKYO.
NEAR THE MONKEY BARS AT THE ELEMENTARY SCHOOL.
KEIKO, THE GIRL FROM THE SOBA SHOP THREE DOORS DOWN...
SHE DID BALLET FOR FIFTEEN YEARS, SO SHE HELPED ME LEARN THE BASICS!
UN!
DEUX!
TROIS!
BOY, WAS SHE TOUGH ON ME!

I STUDIED FOR A WHOLE SIX MONTHS BEFORE I TOOK THE KOUKA TEST.
RAIN OR SHINE...
I WAS AT THE PARK!
THAT SO?
SIX MONTHS, HUH?
BUT I LOVE DOING ARABESQUES! DO YOU WANNA KNOW WHY?!
MAYBE ANOTHER TIME.
IT'S STILL CLASS RIGHT NOW.
HA HA HA!
WHAT ARE YOU DOING OUT HERE?
OH, TAICHI.
I'M EATING LUNCH. OBVIOUSLY.

THE UPPER-CLASSMEN WILL GET MAD AT YOU IF THEY FIND OUT YOU'RE EATING OUT HERE.
I DON'T WANNA EAT LUNCH IN THAT TINY CLASSROOM.
WHY CAN'T FIRST-YEAR STUDENTS TALK OR SMILE OR DO ANY-THING OUTSIDE THEIR CLASS-ROOM?
NO IDEA.
THAT'S JUST HOW IT'S BEEN FOR A HUNDRED YEARS, I GUESS.
IT'S WEIRD! BUT WHAT-EVER.
I DON'T REALLY WANT TO TALK TO PEOPLE, ANYWAY.
SO THAT WORKS OUT FOR ME.
......
HEY, TAICHI?

WHO'S SHIRAKAWA AKIYA?

ASKING ABOUT A BOY? THIS IS NEW.

HE YOUR TYPE?

GLARE

I'M MORE INTO KOUZA-BUROU-SAN MYSELF.

HE'S SO HOT! ♡

HEE HEE!

I *REALLY* DON'T CARE.

CHOMP

YOU KNOW THE HEAD OF THAT SUPER FAMOUS KABUKI TROUPE, SHIRAKAWA KAOU?

SHIRAKAWA AKIYA'S ONE OF HIS STUDENTS AND FOLLOWERS, AS WELL AS THE SON OF KAOU'S COUSIN.

KAOU HIMSELF NEVER HAD ANY SONS, YOU SEE.

SO, RIGHT NOW, AKIYA'S ONE OF THE PEOPLE CLOSEST TO BEING THE 16TH PERSON TO INHERIT THE SHIRAKAWA MANTLE.

DO KABUKI ACTORS HAVE REALLY STRONG CORES?

I'D SAY SO. THEY'VE GOT TO BE PHYSICALLY FIT FOR KABUKI.

HUNH.

EVEN IF SHIRAKAWA AKIYA REALLY IS SARASA'S BOY-FRIEND...
THAT DOESN'T MEAN HE'S THE REASON SHE'S GOT SUCH A STRONG CORE.

YOU'RE ROOMING WITH THAT WATANABE-SAN, RIGHT? HOW'S THAT GOING?
GULP!
YOU TWO FRIENDS YET? SHE'S PRETTY FUNNY!
NO, SHE'S NOT!
SHE'S NOT FUNNY AT ALL!
SARASA...
DOESN'T LISTEN TO WHAT ANYONE ELSE SAYS.
SHE'S LOUD.
SHE'S ALWAYS ROLLING OFF HER BED.
AND SHE SLEEPS IN EVERY DAY!

SUGIMOTO-SAN WON A WHOLE BUNCH OF BALLET CONTESTS BACK IN THE DAY.
WHAAA?! THAT'S AWE-SOME!
HOW LONG HAVE YOU BEEN DOING BALLET?
MY FAMILY RUNS A BALLET SCHOOL, SO SINCE I WAS BORN, BASICALLY.
NO WAY! THAT'S SO CRAZY!

HOW DOES A BABY DO BALLET?!
AH HA HA!
I JUST MEANT THAT I'VE BEEN DOING IT FOR A VERY, VERY LONG TIME!
TWITCH
TWITCH
HUH? IF YOU'RE SO GOOD AT BALLET...

THEN WHY DID YOU WANT TO COME TO KOUKA, INSTEAD OF PURSUING A BALLET CAREER?

THAT'S A DUMB QUES-TION.

IT'S BECAUSE I LIKE KOUKA MORE THAN BALLET DANCING.

OBVIOUSLY.

YOU'RE SO COOL!
YOU'RE JUST THE COOLEST, SUGIMOTO-SAN!

HOW LONG HAVE YOU ALL BEEN DOING BALLET?
TEN YEARS.
SIX.
THREE YEARS.
OH, YOU WANNA HEAR WHY I LIKE--
AH!
NO, THAT SOUNDS ANNOYING, SO WE'RE GONNA PASS ON IT.
BUT *WHYYY?!*
OH! HOW LONG HAVE YOU BEEN DOING BALLET, AI-CHAN?

HUH?

WHERE IS AI-CHAN, ANYWAY?

AND SHE CAN'T READ THE ROOM!

DID I MENTION SHE'S LOUD? *OH, I DID.*

GOD, I WISH I COULD CHANGE ROOMS.

WOW.

YOU'VE CHANGED A LITTLE, AI.
MAYBE IT IS A GOOD THING YOU CAME TO KOUKA.
WHAT'S THAT SUPPOSED TO MEAN?

I MEAN, BEFORE, YOU NEVER TOOK AN INTEREST IN ANYONE BESIDES YOURSELF.
NOT EVEN WHEN YOU WERE IN JPX.
I'M NOT INTERESTED IN HER!

SHE JUST KEEPS FORCING HERSELF INTO MY LIFE.
AI.
SHE'S SO ANNOYING!
SHE REALLY PISSES ME OFF.
I THINK YOU'VE GOT IT ALL WRONG.
I THINK THE TRUTH IS...
YOU CAN'T TAKE YOUR EYES OFF OF HER.

TAICHI.
YOU DON'T GET IT.
CLENCH
YOU DON'T GET HOW...
MYA HA! ♡

HORRIFI-CALLY ANNOYING SHE IS!
GRR! GRR! GRR! GRR!
イライラ
GRR! GRR!
イライラ
I DON'T THINK SHE'S A BAD PERSON.
I HOPE YOU CAN BE FRIENDS WITH HER.
SHWP
スッ
I DON'T NEED FRIENDS.
I'LL TALK TO YOU. THAT'S FINE.
BUT THERE'S NO WAY I COULD EVER BE FRIENDS WITH WATANABE-SAN!

NOT EVER!

OHHH!

AI-CHAN! WHERE'D YOU DISAPPEAR TO?

I THOUGHT YOU MIGHT'VE GONE TO THE BATH-ROOM...

BUT YOU WERE GONE TOO LONG.

UNLESS YOU DIDN'T FEEL WELL?!

I'M FINE.

DID YOU HAVE LUNCH YET?

YEP.

DID YOU EAT ENOUGH? Y'KNOW, I'M ALWAYS WORRIED ABOUT YOU GETTING ENOUGH FOOD!

YOU DON'T NEED TO WORRY ABOUT ME.

AWW, DON'T SAY THAT! WE'RE FRIENDS, AREN'T WE?
FREEZE

NO,
WE'RE
NOT.

KOBE.
I'M FINALLY HERE.
KA-SNAP
SO, THIS IS THE FAMOUS KOUKA HANANO-MICHI.
KA-SNAP
HANANOMICHI
KA-SNAP
AND THAT'S THE KOUKA PERFOR-MANCE HALL.
KOUKA
KA-SNAP
AND THAT'S THE KOUKA SCHOOL OF MUSICAL AND THEATRICAL ARTS.

48
AI
JPX
AI NARATA
KA-SNAP
I WONDER IF I'LL SEE NARAC-CHI...
IF I WAIT HERE LONG ENOUGH.

B-BUT!
BUT WE SHARE THE SAME ROOM!

IF WE'RE NOT FRIENDS, THEN I WANT TO *TRY* TO BE FRIENDS WITH YOU, AI-CHAN!
LOOK.

I DON'T REALLY WANT TO BE FRIENDS...

WITH ANYONE.

B-BUT...
I HATE IT.
DEALING...
WITH PEOPLE ...
IS A PAIN.
THERE'S ONLY ONE REASON I CAME TO KOUKA.

HEY! YOU GIRLS!
YOU'RE FIRST-YEARS, AREN'T YOU?!
IF I JOIN THE KOUKA REVUE AND DO A GOOD JOB, I CAN STAY WITH THEM TILL I'M THIRTY.
YOU KNOW YOU'RE NOT ALLOWED TO TALK IN THE HALLS!
UGH!
AND MOST KOUKA FANS ARE WOMEN.

!
WHAT'S GOING ON?
OH, CLASS REP TAKEI!
THESE GIRLS WERE ARGUING IN THE HALL!
I JUST WANT TO HAVE A PEACEFUL LIFE.
CALL THEIR ADVISORS, RISA AND HIJIRI.
AND MAKE SURE ALL OF CLASS A MEETS UP IN THE AUDITORIUM AFTER CLASS IS OVER TODAY!

I DON'T NEED FRIENDS.
I JUST WANT TO BE AS FAR AWAY AS POSSIBLE FROM THE WORLD OF MEN.
THAT'S ALL I WANT.
I WONDER WHEN...
NARACCHI WILL WALK THIS WAY?

7

THE WORDS "YOU'RE SO PRETTY!" AND "WHAT A CUTIE!"...

HAVE ALWAYS MEANT "HELLO" TO ME.

MY GOODNESS, AI-CHAN! YOU JUST GET CUTER EVERY DAY, DON'T YOU?
WHY, I'D ALMOST THINK YOU WERE A DOLL, YOU'RE SO PRECIOUS!

MY, WHAT A BIG BEAR YOU'VE GOT THERE!
MY DADDY BOUGHT IT FOR ME.

WHA--?!

THAT'S NOT TRUE.

AWW.

REALLY?

WOW!

THAT'S JUST WHAT MY MOM TOLD EVERYONE.

WHICH MEANS IT'S PROBABLY A LIE.

SO... AI-CHAN, SWEETIE?

WHO IS YOUR DADDY?

DON'T KNOW.
THAT IS TRUE.
MY MOTHER...
IS NARATA KIMIKO, A FAMOUS MOVIE STAR.
THE LADIES FROM THE TEAHOUSE HAVE CORNERED AI.
THOSE OLD BIDDIES LOVE TO GOSSIP.

IT MAKES SENSE SHE'S POPULAR. SHE'S A CUTE KID.

I DON'T THINK THAT'S IT.

THEY JUST WANT TO KNOW WHO HER FATHER IS.

I'M ALSO CURIOUS ABOUT THAT.

MY UNCLE TAICHI IS A BALLET DANCER.

THE OLD MAN IN HACHIOJI TOLD ME SOMETHING FUNNY, YOU KNOW.
HE SAID MY LOVING ELDER SISTER AND SWEET YOUNGER BROTHER WERE CHASING DOWN EVERY LAST MAN IN THE DAMN CITY.

MY GRANDMOTHER PASSED AWAY SEVEN YEARS AGO.

SHE LEFT BEHIND A LEGACY OF BEAUTY AND A SUBSTANTIAL FORTUNE.

HEY, NA-RA-TAAA!
YOUR MOM'S SUCH A SLUT!
I SAW HER TITTIES ON TV LAST NIGHT!
HAW HAW!
HER BOOBIES WERE WOBBLING LIKE *THIS!*
UGH! GROW UP, BOYS!
QUIT IT!
GOD, BOYS ARE SOOOO STUPID!
I KNOW!
YOU'RE MAKING AI-CHAN FEEL EMBARRASSED!
OH, NO.
I DON'T CARE.

MY MOM'S WORKING REALLY HARD.
I'M NOT EMBARRASSED BY HER.
THAT'S ALSO A LIE.
THROB!
OH, WOW, AI-CHAN, YOU'RE SO MATURE!!
YOU BOYS ONLY TEASE AI-CHAN BECAUSE YOU LIKE HER, RIGHT?
N-NO!
I'VE NEVER EVEN SEEN ONE OF MY MOTHER'S FILMS.
I'M SURPRISED NARATA-SAN DIDN'T ENROLL HER DAUGHTER IN A PRIVATE SCHOOL.
WELL, WHEN I MET WITH HER...
SHE SAID SHE WANTED AI-CHAN TO LIVE A "NORMAL" LIFE.
PERHAPS BECAUSE SHE'S AN ACTRESS? THEY'RE A WEIRD BUNCH.
FOR ALL HER TALK, SHE SEEMS LIKE A PRETTY HANDS-OFF MOM.
THOUGH SHE DID GET HER DAUGHTER'S HAIR PERMED!
SAID IT MADE HER LOOK EXOTIC!
HUNH.
I DON'T REALLY LIKE BEING BULLIED.
BUT MOM SAYS THAT CUTE GIRLS HAVE TO "TOUGH IT OUT."

IT HAPPENED AROUND THE TIME I WAS WAY BIGGER THAN PAPA BEAR.

THIS IS SEIJI-SAN.
WHO KNOWS, HE MIGHT...

BE YOUR NEW DADDY, AI.

HI THERE, AI-CHAN.
IT SURE IS NICE TO MEET YOU!

I DIDN'T CARE THAT HE "MIGHT" BE MY NEW DAD.
IT'S NICE TO MEET YOU, TOO.
WHY WOULD I WHEN I DIDN'T EVEN CARE ABOUT MY OLD ONE?

MY MOTHER HAD BROUGHT HOME BOY-FRIENDS BEFORE.
BUT THIS ONE WAS DIFFERENT. HE SEEMED MORE... MATURE.
SEIJI-SAN'S A REALLY NICE GUY!
AND YOU KNOW WHAT ELSE?
HE'S GOING TO LIVE WITH US!
FROM THEN ON, THAT MAN WAS IN OUR HOUSE EVERY DAY.
MY MOTHER NEVER TOLD ME MUCH ABOUT HIM...
LIKE WHERE SHE MET HIM...
OR WHAT HE DID FOR A LIVING.
BUT THAT WASN'T STRANGE.
SHE RARELY TOLD ME ANY-THING.
ALMOST ...
YAY! GOT IT!

AI-CHAN.
I CAN SEE YOUR UNDIES.
HEH!
BOY, AI-CHAN!
YOU SURE ARE A CUTIE.
SORRY ABOUT THE WAIT, SEIJI-SAN!
C'MON, LET'S GO.
WATCH THE HOUSE, OKAY, AI?

HIS WORDS SENT A CHILL DOWN MY SPINE.
I DIDN'T KNOW WHY.
I MEAN, MY MOM HAD PICKED HIM OUT.
HE COULDN'T BE THAT BAD. HE NEVER GOT MAD AT ME, EITHER.
SO, WHEN HE WAS WAITING OUTSIDE THE DOOR WHEN I GOT OUT OF THE BATH...
OR ALWAYS STOPPED RIGHT IN FRONT OF MY DOOR WHEN HE WALKED DOWN THE HALL...
I THOUGHT THEY WERE JUST COINCIDENCES.
MY MOTHER...
ALL GROWN-UPS...
KNEW SO MUCH MORE THAN ME.
SO, THEY COULDN'T BE WRONG ABOUT ANYTHING.
OKAY, I'M OFF FOR MY ONE-WEEK LOCATION SHOOT!
BE GOOD NOW.

YOU TWO PLAY NICE, OKAY?
UM? MOM?
GOOD... GOOD LUCK AT YOUR SHOOT!
AND, UH... COME BACK SOON!
OH, C'MON!
YOU'RE A BIG GIRL, AI. DON'T BE SUCH A BABY!
YOU DO AS SEIJI-SAN SAYS, ALL RIGHT?
I'M WORKING MYSELF TO DEATH FOR YOU, YOU KNOW.

IT'S LATE. YOU SHOULD HEAD HOME, AI-CHAN.
AWW.
OKAY.
AI-CHAN!
I MADE SOME CUP-CAKES.
TAKE SOME HOME WITH YOU!
YOUR MOM MAKES CUPCAKES, MIKI-CHAN?!
YUP, SHE SURE DOES!
WOW! THEY'RE NOT FROM A STORE?!
......
......

YOU KNOW, MOM...
AI-CHAN DOESN'T GO ON PLAYDATES VERY OFTEN.
REALLY, NOW?

BOY, SHE SURE IS A CUTE ONE.
RIGHT ?! ☆
I WOULDN'T LET A GIRL LIKE THAT WALK HOME BY HER-SELF!
WHAT ?!
THANK GOOD-NESS YOU'RE PLAIN LIKE ME!
I DON'T ...
WANT TO GO HOME.

HUH...?
THE CHAIN'S ON?
AI-CHAN?
MY! IT'S LATE!
I WAS WORRIED ABOUT YOU.
I DIDN'T KNOW WHAT YOU WANTED TO EAT...
SO, I ORDERED A WHOLE BUNCH OF DIFFERENT THINGS.
SORRY.
IT'S ALL RIGHT. C'MON, LET'S EAT.
N-NO THANKS.
I'M JUST GONNA EAT THE CUPCAKE MIKI-CHAN'S MOM MADE.
I'LL DO MY HOME-WORK AND GO TO BED.

IS THAT SO? WELL, I SUPPOSE THERE'S NO USE TRYING TO CHANGE YOUR MIND.
I'M JUST TRYING TO BE FRIENDS WITH YOU, AI-CHAN.
AH...
W-WE ARE FRIENDS!

REALLY?
WHY DON'T YOU PROVE IT?
COME GIVE ME A KISS.

HUH?
A KISS?

FRIENDS GIVE EACH OTHER KISSES?
OH, I GUESS TAICHI KISSED ME WHEN I WAS LITTLE...
YOU'RE JUST THE CUTEST, AI! ♡
UGH! SO ANNOY-ING!

O-OKAY.
UM.
BUT...
HEH!
OH, MY CUTE AI-CHAN,
YOU'RE SUCH A GOOD GIRL.
HUH?

WHAT'S HE...?

THUMP

HAAAAH.

WHAT'S HE DOING?

HAAAAH.

HAAAAH.

GROSS.
GROSS.
GROSS.

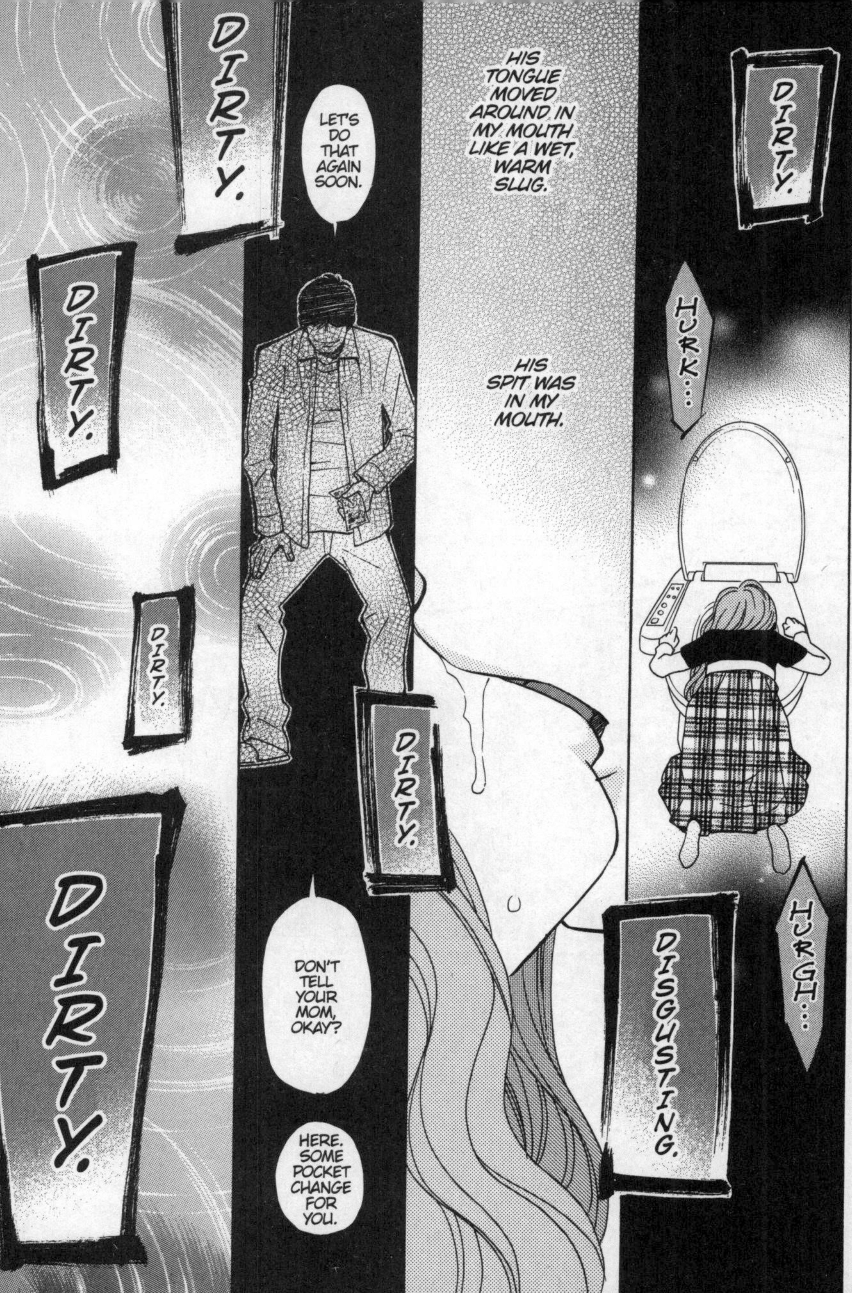
DIRTY.
HURK...
HURGH...
DISGUSTING.
HIS TONGUE MOVED AROUND IN MY MOUTH LIKE A WET, WARM SLUG.
HIS SPIT WAS IN MY MOUTH.
LET'S DO THAT AGAIN SOON.
DIRTY.
DON'T TELL YOUR MOM, OKAY?
HERE. SOME POCKET CHANGE FOR YOU.
DIRTY.
DIRTY.
DIRTY.
DIRTY.

HE MADE ME DIRTY.
DOES THIS... DOES THIS MAKE ME A "SLUT"?
WHAT DID THE BOYS IN MY CLASS SAY?
You know what happens to slutty girls?
They get pregnant!
NO, NO, NO! I CAN'T HAVE A BABY!
WHAT IF MY TUMMY GETS ALL BIG?
MAYBE IF I SQUEEZE IT REAL TIGHT, IT WON'T GET BIG...
BRRRRNG BRRRNG
CLICK
MOM
090XXXXXXXX
HELLO? AI?

WHAT IS IT? I'M IN THE MIDDLE OF A SHOOT.
MOM.
PLEASE.
PLEASE COME HOME, JUST... *PLEASE!*
GOD. YOU'VE BEEN SUCH A BABY LATELY, YOU KNOW?
YOU'RE IN FIFTH GRADE, SWEETIE!
BUT I'M SCARED OF HIM!
OF WHO? SEIJI-SAN?
HE'S ALWAYS STARING AT ME.
AND... AND HE WAITS FOR ME IN FRONT OF MY ROOM...
A-AND...
UGH, AI. YOU'RE MAKING A FUSS OVER NOTHING.
I DON'T HAVE TIME FOR THIS.
B-BUT TODAY...
HE...
LOOK, AI.

WHAT ON EARTH AM I SUPPOSED TO DO...
WITH A LITTLE GIRL LIKE YOU?!

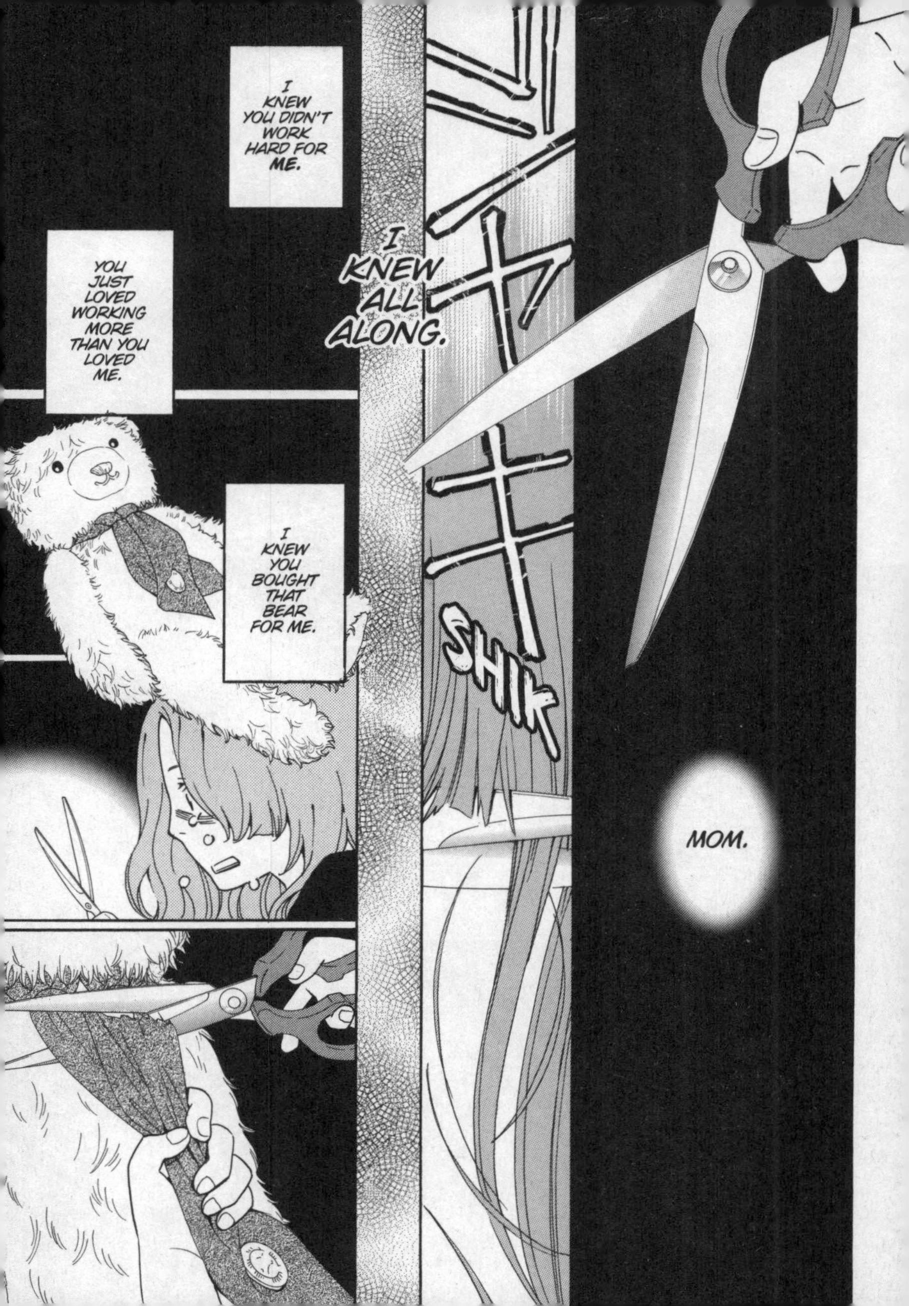
I KNEW YOU DIDN'T WORK HARD FOR ME.
YOU JUST LOVED WORKING MORE THAN YOU LOVED ME.
I KNEW YOU BOUGHT THAT BEAR FOR ME.
I KNEW ALL ALONG.
SHIK
MOM.

YOU'RE AN ACTRESS.
MY DAD ISN'T AROUND.
IF I'M NOT PERFECT, EVERYONE WILL GOSSIP ABOUT YOU.
THAT'S WHY I PRETENDED TO BE A HAPPY LITTLE GIRL.
I LIED TO EVERY-ONE AND STUFFED ALL THOSE FEELINGS DOWN INSIDE.
BUT NOW, I'M GOING TO RIP THEM OUT AND MAKE MYSELF TOTALLY EMPTY.
"I WON'T BE LONELY!"
"I'LL BE FINE!"
"I LOVE MY BEAR!"
"MY DADDY GOT IT FOR ME!"
"MOMMY?"
"HEY, MOMMY!"

NOW, NOBODY CAN STUFF ANY-THING ELSE INSIDE ME.
NOT EVEN ME.
"I LOVE YOU, MOMMY!"
OUR NEXT GUEST IS FAMOUS ACTRESS, NARATA KIMIKO-SAN!
I HAVE TO SAY, THAT RISQUÉ SCENE IN YOUR MOST RECENT WORK? UN-BUH-LIEVABLE!
HOW DOES YOUR DAUGHTER FEEL ABOUT IT? DOES SHE GET EMBAR-RASSED?
WELL, I ONLY DO NUDE SCENES FOR FILMS I FEEL HAVE A HIGH ARTISTIC QUALITY TO THEM.
MY DAUGHTER'S A SMART LITTLE GIRL. SHE UNDER-STANDS.

GA-CHAK
AI?
YOU AWAKE?
Love
3

WHAT HAPPENED TO YOUR HAIR?
ARE YOU OKAY?
SHAKE SHAKE
DO YOU WANT ME TO DO ANYTHING?
P-PUT...
A LOCK ON MY DOOR.

IT TOOK EVERYTHING I HAD JUST TO ASK THAT OF HIM.
MY MOTHER RETURNED SEVERAL DAYS LATER.
UGH!
SHUT UP!
GOD, YOU ARE JUST LIKE MOM!
SHE GOT INTO A BIG FIGHT WITH TAICHI WHEN HE CAME OVER TO VISIT.

C'MERE, AI.
I'LL GIVE YOU A MAGIC WAND.

IT'S A KEY TO MY HOUSE.

YOU CAN VISIT ANYTIME, EVEN IF I'M NOT HOME.
IF YOU CAN'T STAND IT HERE ANYMORE, OR SOMETHING BAD HAPPENS...

YOU CAN ESCAPE TO MY PLACE.
THE YEARS WENT BY.
SOON, I WAS IN JUNIOR HIGH.
THE MAN KEPT LEECHING OFF MY MOTHER.
WHETHER IT WAS THE LOCK TAICHI PUT ON MY DOOR OR SOMETHING ELSE...
HE DIDN'T LAY A FINGER ON ME AFTER THAT.
AND I LEARNED THAT YOU CAN'T GET PREGNANT FROM KISSING.
BUT WITH HIM IN THE HOUSE, I NEVER FELT SAFE.
THE KIDS STARTED TO CALL ME "NOH MASK" BECAUSE OF HOW STONE-FACED I WAS.
EVERYONE STARTED SAYING I WAS NO FUN AND STOPPED BEING MY FRIEND.
NOT THAT I CARE IF I HAVE FRIENDS OR NOT.

THE FEWER FRIENDS I HAD, THE MORE MEN STARTED TO STARE AT ME ON THE STREET.
I HATE MEN WHO EXPECT TO GET SOME-THING OUT OF ME.
PIGS.
I WISH ALL MEN WOULD DIE.
THESE THOUGHTS WERE MY SHIELD.
I STARED DAGGERS AT EACH AND EVERY ONE OF THEM, DAY IN, DAY OUT.
TAICHI CAN LIVE, I GUESS.
Kuroge Shun
JPX
Producer
JPX48?

YES. IT'S AN IDOL GROUP I'M PRODUCING.
HAIRY HANDS.
IT'S A GROUP OF FORTY-EIGHT GIRLS, AGES FOURTEEN AND UP.
MORE IF YOU COUNT OUR PROVISIONAL OR "TEMPORARY" MEMBERS.
WHEN I SAW YOUR DAUGHTER, NARATA-SAN, I KNEW SHE'D BE PERFECT!
I COULDN'T DISAGREE MORE. LOOK AT HER! SHE'S JUST NOT THE *TYPE*.
SHE WAS A *LOT* MORE FEMININE WHEN SHE WAS YOUNGER, BUT NOW, WELL...
HEH.
AN ALL-GIRL GROUP?
FORTY-EIGHT OF THEM?
THAT'S WHY SHE'S PERFECT! WE WANT **VARIETY!**
A COOL, LEVEL-HEADED GIRL LIKE AI-SAN WOULD BE A WONDERFUL ADDITION TO OUR GROUP.
SHE CAN START BY JUST ATTENDING SOME SESSIONS, LIKE IT'S AN AFTER-SCHOOL CLUB.
THOUGH OF COURSE, WHEN THINGS GET BUSY, SHE'LL HAVE TO TAKE TIME OFF SCHOOL.
OUR MAIN STUDIO'S IN AKIHABARA.
AKIBA ...?

I'LL DO IT!

All in!

EH?

GREAT!

THERE WON'T BE ANY MEN.

AND TAICHI LIVES CLOSE TO AKIBA.

IF I DO THIS...

I CAN MOVE AWAY FROM HOME.

I WAS SO STUPID.

I DIDN'T EVEN STOP TO THINK ABOUT...

THE **TARGET AUDIENCE** OF AN ALL-GIRL IDOL GROUP.

LATER...

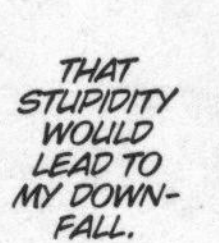
THAT STUPIDITY WOULD LEAD TO MY DOWNFALL.

Let go, creep.

Chapter 8

HEY, NARACCHI?

HEY, SO...

WHY DO YOU ALWAYS PUSH PEOPLE AWAY?

YOU DO EVERYTHING RIGHT, BUT YOU DON'T GO ABOVE AND BEYOND.

MOST OF THE TIME, IT SEEMS LIKE YOU DON'T EVEN WANT TO BE HERE.

BUT YOU'RE STILL ALWAYS PICKED TO PERFORM.

SOME OF THE OTHER GIRLS ARE STARTING TO TRASH-TALK YOU BECAUSE OF IT.

AS A TEAM LEADER, I WANT TO HELP YOU FIT INTO THE GROUP BETTER.

THAT, AND I WANT TO BE BETTER FRIENDS WITH YOU, TOO!

SO, I WAS JUST WONDERING IF YOU COULD TELL ME WHY YOU KEEP TO YOURSELF ALL THE TIME.

WELL...

I WAS MOLESTED WHEN I WAS LITTLE.
IT'S BEEN HARD FOR ME TO TRUST PEOPLE SINCE THEN.
8

THERE WASN'T A DEEP REASON...

FOR *WHY* I TOLD HER.

I JUST WANTED TO SEE WHAT WOULD CHANGE ...

UHH... OH...

HE JUST FORCED ME TO KISS HIM, BUT STILL.

IF I TOLD SOME-ONE.

I WANTED TO KNOW IF SOME-THING *WOULD* CHANGE.

O-OH! IS THAT ALL?

PHEW!

AH, WOW. I...I WASN'T EXPECTING THAT.

BUT THERE ARE LOTS OF GIRLS OUT THERE...

WHO HAVE GONE THROUGH *WAY* WORSE THAN THAT.

SO...IT MIGHT BE BEST IF YOU JUST LET IT GO AND MOVED ON, YOU KNOW?

TRAUMA ...
IS SUPPOSED TO MAKE YOU STRONGER COMPARED TO OTHERS.
OR AM I SUPPOSED TO BE COMFORTED KNOWING THAT THERE ARE PEOPLE WHO EXPERIENCED WORSE THINGS THAN I DID?
OKAY? ♡
SHE MEANT WELL. SHE WAS JUST REALLY DEVOTED TO HER JOB.
I SHOULDN'T HAVE SAID ANY-THING.
YEAH.
SORRY. IT WAS JUST A JOKE.
TALKING TO PEOPLE...
DOESN'T MAKE YOU FEEL BETTER.
THAT WAS WHAT I LEARNED THAT DAY.
ARGH! I CAN'T BELIEVE HER!

THAT GIRL!
SHE MUST'VE SAID *SOMETHING* TO YOU AGAIN!
WHY ELSE WOULD YOU BE THAT MAD AT HER?

PLUS, THANKS TO HER, WE HAD TO STAND IN THE HALL AND LECTURE CLASS A!
AND NOW WE'VE GOT TO SUPERVISE YOU TWO FOR THE EXTRA HOUR OF MORNING CLEANING YOU'RE DOING THE NEXT TWO DAYS? *GAH!*

I'M SORRY, SENPAI. I DIDN'T WANT TO CAUSE YOU TROUBLE.
IT'S MY FAULT, ANYWAY.

YOU REALLY ARE NICE...
NARATA-SAN.

DON'T YOU WORRY ABOUT ME, OKAY?

I'M YOUR ASSIGNED SENPAI, SO IF YOU'VE GOT ANY ISSUES, FEEL FREE TO VENT TO ME.

IF WATANABE-SAN BOTHERS YOU AGAIN, TELL ME, AND I'LL DO SOMETHING ABOUT IT.

OH!

SHFF
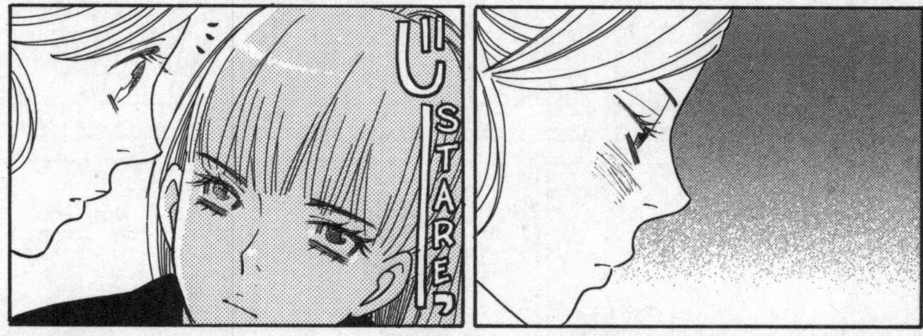
STARE

HMPH!

RISA-SENPAI! THAT CUTE SENPAI JUST "HMPHED" ME!
AAAAHHHH!

I DIDN'T EVEN DO ANY-THING!

ALL RIGHT, GIRLS! GOT YOUR TAP SHOES ON?

HEE HEE! TAP SHOES ARE SO FUNNY!

I LIKE THE WAY THEY SOUND.

WHEN YOU TAP DANCE, YOU PRODUCE SOUNDS WITH THE TOE, BALL, AND HEEL OF YOUR TAP SHOE.

TOE

BALL

HEEL

FEEL THE RHYTHM IN YOUR BODY.

BY MIXING AND COMBINING THESE SOUNDS TO A RHYTHM, YOU BECOME A MUSICAL INSTRUMENT AS YOU DANCE.

NOW, LET'S START WITH A BALL-HEEL STEP.

BALL-HEEL!
BALL-HEEL!
HEEL, HEEL!
TAP, TAP, TAP-TAP TAP!
TAP, TAP, TAP-TAP TAP!
STAMP!
NOW, ADD THE TOE.
GLARE
HERE WE GO!
SHUFFLE.
STEP.
BRUSH.
MAKE IT FLOW!
OKAY, NOW, REPEAT AFTER ME...

WHOA!
MY FEET ARE SLIPPING!
GRR! IT WON'T MAKE THE RIGHT SOUND!
I CAN'T REMEMBER THE STEPS...

INTENSE
YOU'VE GOT A GOOD MEMORY, NARATA.
TAP
TAP-
TAP-
TAP
THE SOUND'S A LITTLE OFF, BUT YOU'VE GOT THE ROUTINE DOWN PERFECTLY.
SLIP!
CRACK!

FOCUSED
THOUGH I SHOULDN'T BE SURPRISED, GIVEN YOUR BACK-GROUND.
TAP!
TAP-
TAP-
TAP

BAM!
BA-
BA-
BA-
BAM
TURN!
WATA-NABE.
YOU'RE TOO LOUD.
WHAAAAAAA?!

RHYTHM TAP MIGHT CALL FOR YOUR MOVES TO BE MORE FORCEFUL.

BUT YOU GIRLS ARE LEARNING **BROADWAY** TAP.

YOUR STEPS LOOK LIKE THEY'RE SLAMMING DOWN ONTO THE FLOOR, LIKE THEY'RE HEAVY.

IMAGINE THEY'RE BEING SUCKED INTO THE FLOOR INSTEAD. LET THEM FALL GENTLY.

......

NARATA-SENSEI TOLD ME SOMETHING LIKE THAT, TOO!

HE SAID THAT BECAUSE I'M SO MUCH BIGGER THAN OTHER PEOPLE, I HAVE MORE MASS, SO GRAVITY--

HM? HEY!

YOU! YAMADA!!

HUH? M-ME?!
DID I MESS UP?
NO.
YOU'VE GOTTEN FATTER, HAVEN'T YOU?

U-UHH, WELL...
I *HAVE* GAINED A LITTLE WEIGHT SINCE STARTING SCHOOL...
BAM
A LITTLE? TRY A TON.

BUT, SENSEI! GIRLS ARE CUTER IF THEY'VE GOT A LITTLE JIGGLE TO THEM!
RIGHT?!
WHAT ARE YOU GOING ON ABOUT?!
A *MAN* MIGHT LIKE THAT, BUT NOT US!

THE AUDIENCES YOU'LL PERFORM FOR ARE GOING TO BE PREDOMINANTLY WOMEN.

AND WOMEN HAVE EXTREMELY SHREWD EYES FOR THESE THINGS!

KOUKA FANS WANT TO EXPERIENCE A WORLD OF FANTASY UNLIKE THEIR OWN.

THEY WANT TO SEE A BEAUTY THEY CAN NEVER HOPE TO ACHIEVE!

IT'S ONE OF THE RULES OF KOUKA!

NO FATTIES.

IF YOU WANT TO STAY HERE, SHED THOSE POUNDS!

URK!

FIRST-YEARS

BETTER SHAPE UP, YAMADA, OR YOUR FAT ASS IS OUT OF HERE.

HOSHINO-SAN! YAMADA-SAN'S ALREADY CRYING!

BE NICE TO HER, GOT IT?!

I... I'LL NEVER EAT AGAIN, I SWEAR!
NO! YOU'LL DIE! YOU JUST HAVE TO EAT A LITTLE LESS!

SENSEI SAID YOU COULD LOSE A KILOGRAM A MONTH AND THAT'D BE ENOUGH!

LET'S TALK TO THE R.A. AND SEE IF SHE CAN HELP!

WHY IS SHE LIKE THAT?!
SHE JUST BUTTS INTO PEOPLE'S BUSINESS WHENEVER SHE FEELS LIKE IT!
SHE'S SO ANNOY-ING.
SHE NEEDS TO KEEP HER NOSE OUT OF THINGS.
JOLT

DO YOU...
REMEMBER ME?
WATANABE-SAN!
HAVE YOU SEEN AI AROUND?
NOPE.
SHE MIGHT'VE GONE BACK TO THE DORM.
WATA-NABE-SAN?
SMILE
PLEASE TRY AND BE FRIENDS WITH AI.

BUT AI-CHAN TOLD ME I'M NOT HER FRIEND!
YOU KNOW THAT, RIGHT, NARATA-SENSEI?
HOW AM I SUPPOSED TO BE FRIENDS WITH HER...
AFTER SHE SAID THAT RIGHT TO MY FACE?
TMP
TMP
TMP
TMP
HEY, FIRST-YEAR!
NO RUNNING IN THE HALLS!!

AI? WHAT'S WRONG?

THE GUY I CALLED A CREEP AT THAT FAN EVENT.
H-HE...
HE FOLLOWED ME HERE.
I CAN'T ...
IT'S OKAY. I'LL GET THE TEACHERS TO HANDLE IT.
I'LL WALK YOU BACK TO THE DORM FOR NOW.
BUT I THOUGHT YOU HAD TO HEAD INTO TOKYO FOR WORK, NARATA-SENSEI?
YEAH, BUT THIS IS MORE IMPORT-ANT.
BUT THERE ARE SOOO MANY PEOPLE WHO CAN'T WAIT TO SEE YOU DANCE!
I KNOW!
I'LL WALK HER BACK!
PROBLEM SOLVED!

ARE YOU OKAY?

I HEAR THAT SINGING CAN HELP WHEN YOU'RE SCARED!

OOH! HOW 'BOUT A MATSUDA SEIKO* SONG?!

OKAY! THANKS A BUNCH!

TAICHI !!

*Matsuda Seiko is a popular J-idol from the '80s.

OH!
Let go, creep.
Let go.
BA-THUMP

SQUEEZE
HEY, YOU!
WHAT DO YOU THINK YOU'RE DOING, STALKING A HELPLESS GIRL LIKE THIS?!

I KNOW AI-CHAN'S SUPER CUTE!

BUT SHE'S A STUDENT AT THIS NORMAL...ER, NOT-SO-NORMAL SCHOOL NOW, OKAY?!

SEE?! JUST READ THAT SIGN!!

NOTICE
Due to increased traffic on this path, loitering and/or asking Kouka students for autographs in this area is strictly prohibited. By order of the Kobe Police, City of Kobe, and the Kouka School of Musical and Theatrical Arts

NOTICE
Due to increased traffic on this path, loitering and/or asking Kouka students for autographs in this area is strictly prohibited. By order of the Kobe Police, City of Kobe, and the Kouka School of Musical and Theatrical Arts

FIRST, UH...
HERE. YOU DROPPED THIS EARLIER, NARACCHI.

HER BAG?

HERE YOU GO!
ビクッ
FLINCH

I'M SCARED...!
NO!
I'M SCARED!
I'M SO SCARED!
GRIP
GO...

GO AWAA-AAAY!
DO YOU HATE ME...
BECAUSE I...
I WAS MEAN TO YOU?!
ARE YOU HERE TO GET BACK AT ME?!!

U-UM!
I JUST WANT TO SAY...!
DASH
AH!
AI-CHAN!

YOU'RE GONNA LEAVE POOR, HELPLESS ME ALL BY MYSELF OUT HERE?!
......

U-UMM? YOU DON'T SEEM ALL THAT HELPLESS...

I DON'T NEED SOME STALKER CREEP TELLING *ME* THAT!
FLINCH

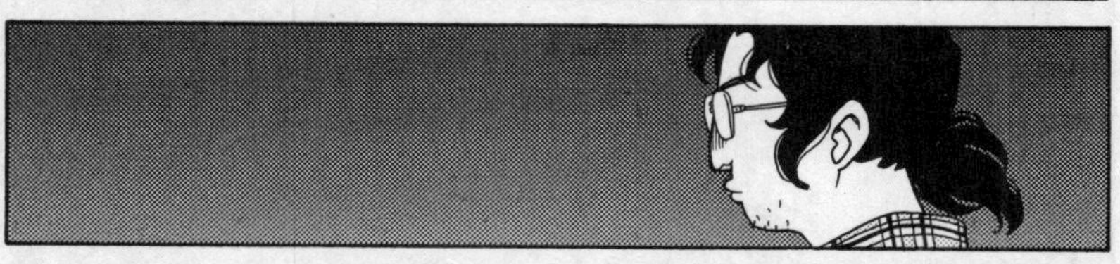

STALKER CREEP...?
YEAH, I GUESS THAT'S WHAT I AM.

UUH
YOU...
YOU'VE GOT IT ALL WRONG ...
ALL I WANTED...
WAS TO APOLOGIZE TO HER!
WAH!

9

*Poster: The Rose of Versailles Manga: Shonen Jump

IT'S ...

IT'S ALL MY FAULT.

IT'S MY FAULT SHE HAD TO QUIT JPX.

HUH?

WHAT DOES THAT MEAN?

MUTTER

MUTTER

MUTTER

I GUESS I WOULDN'T MIND...

HEARING YOU OUT.

MUTTER

MUTTER

MUTTER

SEEING AS I'M AI-CHAN'S ROOM-MATE--

FWOOSH
WHOA, WHOA! NO SHARING PERSONAL INFO!!
NARATA-SENSEI! I THOUGHT YOU HEADED OUT FOR TOKYO!
NO WAY!
I WOULDN'T RUN OFF AND LEAVE YOU TWO ALONE! NOT IN THIS SITUATION!
WHO KNOWS WHAT KIND OF PERVERT WAS WAITING FOR YOU?
HE'S NOT A PERVERT!
HE'S JUST A STALKER!
I'D SAY STALKERS FALL WITHIN THE BOUNDS OF "PERVERTS."
WAIT, REALLY?!

LOOK.
PERVERT, STALKER, EITHER'S FINE WITH ME.
I'M IN THE WRONG, AND I APOLOGIZE. MAY I PLEASE LEAVE?
WAIT, PLEASE! I STILL WANT TO HEAR WHAT YOU HAVE TO SAY!
YOU SEE...
AI-CHAN TOLD ME WE'RE NOT FRIENDS.
AND...
THAT HURTS, BUT DESPITE IT ALL, I STILL...

I STILL WANT TO BE A BETTER FRIEND TO HER!
SO PLEASE, TALK TO ME, MISTER STALKER!
I'M NARATA AI'S UNCLE AND TEACHER.
I'D LIKE TO HEAR WHAT YOU HAVE TO SAY, TOO.

WATA-NABE?
AND A MAN?!

IS THAT HER BOYFRIEND?! HE'S SUCH AN UGGO!
THOUGH IT MAKES SENSE SHE'D HOOK UP WITH SOME WEIRDO.
OH!

HUNH. NARATA-SENSEI'S THERE, TOO.

......

UMM, I DUNNO WHAT TO TELL YOU.
MOST OF IT IS OUT IN THE OPEN ALREADY.
BUT, WELL...

I WAS A NEET*, AND A SHUT-IN, TOO...
YOU'RE A NEET?! COOL!

IN SCHOOL, I WAS NEVER GOOD AT TALKING TO PEOPLE, SO ONE DAY, I JUST STOPPED GOING.
HIS VOICE IS SO ANNOYING!
HE'S GOT THE WORST B.O. IN CLASS!
I STAYED HOME AND SPENT ALL DAY WATCHING ANIME, PLAYING GAMES, AND BROWSING THE INTERNET.
OOH! I LOVE ANIME, TOO!

*NEET: An acronym meaning "not in education, employment, or training."

RIGHT NOW I'M SUPER INTO *ATTACK ON--*
HEY!
LET HIM TELL HIS STORY, WATANABE-SAN.
THEN, ONE DAY, I WAS WATCHING A MUSIC SHOW ON TV.
BLAH
BLAH

JPX
48
THAT WAS WHEN...
I FIRST SAW HER.

WHAT?!
WHO IS SHE?!

WHY DOES SHE...
TRY SO HARD...

TO NEVER, EVER SMILE?!!
ALL THE OTHER GIRLS WERE GRINNING AS HARD AS THEY COULD.
YET HERE WAS THIS FIRST-CLASS IDOL, NOT SMILING AT ALL.
I WAS TOTALLY TAKEN ABACK.
FANS CALLED HER A ROBOT.

LIKE... SHE DIDN'T SEEM SCARED, OR SHY, OR EVEN LONELY. SHE WAS LIKE A PRINCESS FROM A FANTASY WORLD WHO COULD CONTROL ICE AND WINTER, OR LIKE HOMURA FROM *MADO*--
WE GOT IT!

THEN... THERE WAS THAT FATEFUL, UNFORGETTABLE DAY.

TODAY, WE'VE BROUGHT A BUNCH OF YOUR FAVORITE LOCAL MASCOTS TO MEET THE MEMBERS OF JPX!
KOMOMO-CHAN, WHICH ONE DO YOU LIKE?
OH, WOW! LET'S SEE...
......
TAP
SNRK...

I KNEW 100%
WHOOM
SHE'D FALLEN FROM HEAVEN!

Anonymous
Omg Naracch

Anonymous
IT'S A MIR

Anonymous
Did you se
her smile?

Anonymous
DUDE NO

Anonymous
WHOAAAAAA

Anonymous
YESYESYESYESYESYES

Anonymous
LONG HAVE WE WAITED

Anonymous
I PLEDGE MYSELF TO THE NATION OF NARACCHI

Anonymous
Naracchi is soooo cute!!!

Anonymous
Did you see that smile?!

THAT DAY, JUNE 23RD, WAS THE FOUNDING OF THE NARACCHI NATION!

WOW, LOOK AT THOSE BAND-WAGONERS!

SEEING HER LIKE THAT GAVE ME THE COURAGE TO LEAVE MY ROOM.
SOON, I WAS ABLE TO VISIT THE OUTSIDE WORLD AGAIN.

JPX4
JPX-48
I DIDN'T NEED TO WORRY ABOUT WHAT OTHERS THOUGHT OF ME.
I COULD BE MYSELF.

I MADE FRIENDS AND STARTED A PART-TIME JOB.
DID YOU SEE THE SHOW YESTER-DAY?
NARAC-CHI WAS SO CUTE!
YES, YES.

JPX CDS COME WITH SPECIAL BONUSES.
TOKIO DOME

IF YOU BUY ONE OF THEIR CDS, EVEN NORMAL PEOPLE LIKE ME CAN MEET A TOP IDOL IN THE FLESH!
Narata Ai
Session 2
10:30-12:00
No entry after 11:40
ISN'T THAT INCREDIBLE?!

I WANTED TO THANK HER.
Hey, Naracchi!
Thank you for coming.
What did you eat today?!
A plain rice ball. Thank you.

Sheesh. No need to be rude.
I WANTED TO EXPRESS MY GRATITUDE.

I THOUGHT, HOW CAN I TELL HER EVERYTHING...
IN THE BRIEF MOMENT WE'LL SHARE TOGETHER?

WILL I BE ABLE TO...
TELL HER HOW I FEEL?

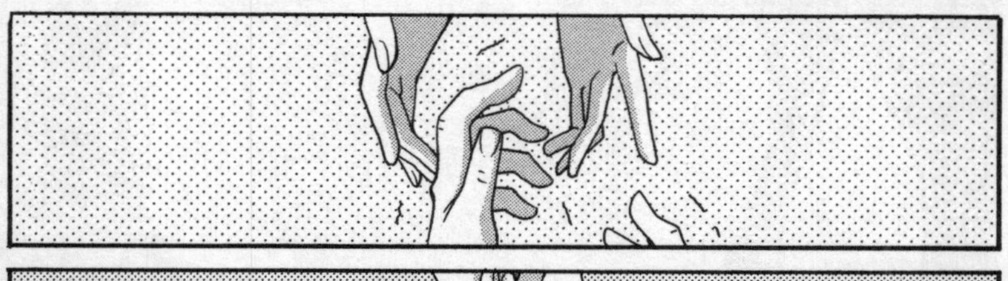

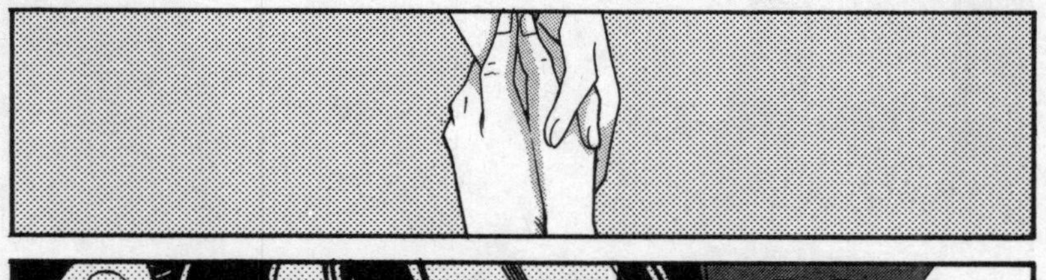

ドキ
BA-DMP
N-Naracchi.
I...
I love you...!
ドキドキ
BA-DMP
BA-DMP

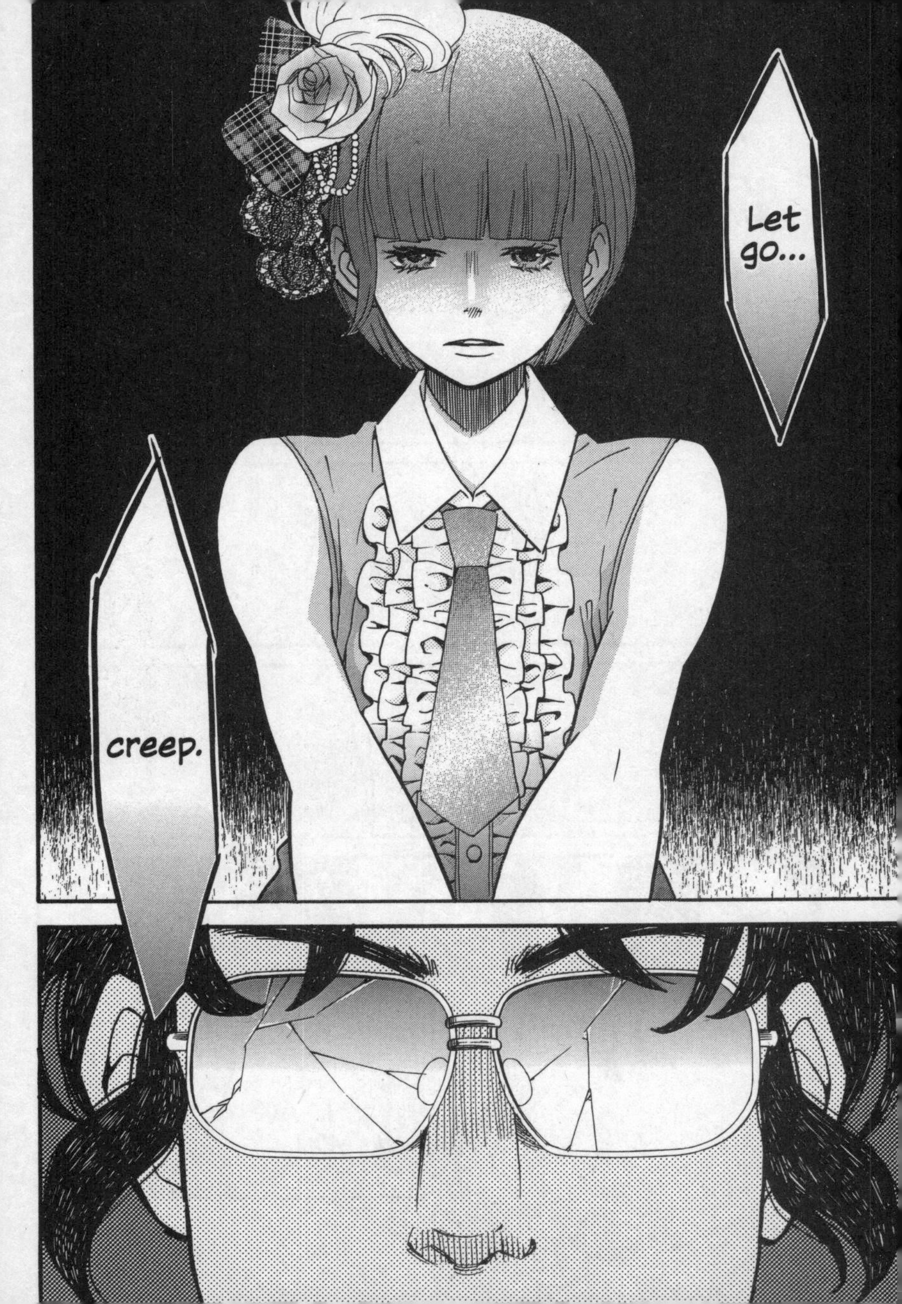
Let go...
creep.

WHAPISH
IT TOOK SO LONG TO CRAWL MY WAY UPWARDS.
BUT IT ONLY TOOK A SECOND...
TO SEND ME BACK INTO THE PITS OF DESPAIR.

I FINALLY REMEMBERED THE TRUTH.
"THAT'S RIGHT. I'M JUST A GROSS OTAKU."
!!
IT'S NOT YOUR FAULT, MR. GROSS OTAKU!

I FEEL SO BAD FOR YOU, MR. GROSS OTAKU!
HUH?
CHEER UP, GROSS MAN!
UH, THANKS?
UH, SURE.
D-DON'T WORRY ABOUT ME, THOUGH.

JPX'S Narata Ai
Lashes Out at Fan
IT ALL HAPPENED BECAUSE I HELD ONTO NARACCHI'S HAND TOO LONG.
BUT I WAS JUST ONE GUY. THERE WAS NOTHING I COULD DO.
NARATA AI CAST OUT OF JPX
BUT I KNEW I HAD TO APOLOGIZE.
THAT INCIDENT GOT LEAKED TO THE FANS OF THE OTHER JPX MEMBERS.
IT QUICKLY GOT OUT OF HAND.
[Naracchi tells JPX fan he's a "creep"]
Anonymous
Whoa, dude, this literally happened?
nymous
ome the haters
nous
appen lmaooooo
ous
wwo creeps
TO MAKE UP FOR IT, NARACCHI WAS FORCED TO GRADUATE THE GROUP WITHOUT A CEREMONY OR ANYTHING.
I HAD TO APOLOGIZE TO HER.
BUT...THAT JUST MAKES ME EVEN MORE OF A CREEP TO NARACCHI, DOESN'T IT? EVEN NOW, I'M JUST HURTING HER ALL OVER AGAIN.

OKAY, I THINK I GET IT.
YOU'RE NOT A BAD PERSON, UH...

MR. CREEPY OTAKU!
YUP, CREEPY OTAKU!
SURE. I GUESS I DESERVE THAT...

I'VE GOT GOOD NEWS AND BAD NEWS.

FIRST, THE GOOD NEWS.
AI DOESN'T HATE YOU SPECIFI-CALLY.
SHE GETS CREEPED OUT BY EVERY MAN. IT'S NOT YOU, IT'S MEN IN GENERAL.
WHA ?!

SHE SAID "CREEP" NOT BECAUSE SHE THINKS YOU'RE A CREEP...
BUT BECAUSE SHE WAS CREEPED OUT.

HERE'S THE BAD NEWS.
AI ISN'T AS EMOTIONALLY ATTACHED TO JPX AS YOU MIGHT WANT HER TO BE.

AND, SADLY...
I CAN SAY THE SAME THING ABOUT HER ATTACHMENT TO KOUKA.

AT SOME POINT IN HER LIFE...
AI DETACHED HERSELF EMOTION-ALLY FROM EVERY-THING.
IT'S LIKE SHE DECIDED NOT TO CARE ABOUT ANYTHING ANYMORE.

THAT, OR SHE JUST STOPPED SHOWING HER FEELINGS TO ANYONE.

FOR SELF-DEFENSE

TEAR SPRAY

PROTECT YOURSELF!

GRAB

I THINK RIGHT NOW, SHE'S TRYING TO FIND A PLACE WHERE SHE CAN RELAX AND FEEL SAFE.

"DEALING WITH PEOPLE...
"IS A PAIN."

IT SEEMS LIKE SUCH A WASTE.
THERE ARE LOTS OF PEOPLE WHO TRY TO GET INTO KOUKA AND DON'T.

I KNOW.
SHE *DOES* LIKE TO SING AND DANCE, I CAN TELL YOU THAT.

THE FIRST TIME...
I SAW AI-CHAN...
I THOUGHT...
SHE LOOKED LIKE ALICE STUMBLING INTO WONDER-LAND.

"HOW PERFECT FOR KOUKA," I THOUGHT.

THE KOUKA STAGE...
AND ALL OF ITS DAZZLING LIGHTS...

WOULD SHINE SO PERFECTLY...
ON SOME-ONE LIKE HER.

OH, NARATA-SAN!

WHERE ARE YOU GOING?

IT'S ALMOST TIME FOR DINNER.

WATANABE-SAN'S NOT BACK YET...

I'M GOING TO GO LOOK FOR HER.

WATA-NABE-SAN? OH...

I THINK I SAW HER ON MY WAY OVER HERE.
SHE WAS SITTING ALONE WITH SOME GUY...
I THINK HE WAS HER BOY-FRIEND?

OH!
NEVER MIND.
IT WAS PROBABLY SOMEONE ELSE.

EXCUSE ME!
DASH

HIJIRI, WHAT'RE YOU DOING THERE?
OH, NOTHING.
DINNER'S READY.
I KNOW.
HEE HEE!
WHAT A GREAT PIC. ♡

NOW, THEN.
WHAT SHOULD I DO WITH IT?
BACK THEN...
I REALLY WANTED...

TO STAND ON THAT STAGE WITH HER.
I WANTED IT...
WITH ALL MY HEART.
SWG

HAAH!
HAAH!

SHE'S GONE! OH, JEEZ! WHAT NOW?
DID THAT GUY DO SOME-THING TO HER?!

AH HA HA HA HA HA HA!

RUSTLE

KAGEKI SHOJO!!

The Curtain Rises

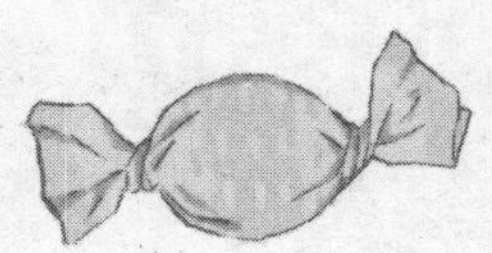

KAGEKI SHOJO!!

The Curtain Rises

90%
10:21
iPad
Sarasa @sara3
@jiraiya-bot I made someone I like angry and she told me she hated me.
I don't understand.
I went out to the field today and

Chapter 10

Sarasa @sara3
@jiraiya-bot She told me before we're not even friends, and now she says she hates me. It's pretty bad.

HMM.

EVEN SO, I STILL...

10

あははは
BWA HA HA HA!
HAI!
HAI!
HAI!
HAI!
AH HA HA!
あーはは
HAI!
HAI!
HAI!
HAI!
I MEAN, YOUR MOVES ARE SHARP, BUT I THINK YOU'RE JUST PUTTING WAY TOO MUCH FORCE INTO THEM!
FUNNY AS HELL, THOUGH!
YOU'RE NOT HALF BAD.
WELL, I AM THE RISING STAR OF KOUKA, AFTER ALL!

STRETCH

LIKE *THIS?*

OH!
AI-CHAN!
YOU CAME BACK!
WHAT'S UP?
"WHAT'S UP?"
YOU...
HUH? WHAT'D YOU SAY?
I REALLY...

I REALLY, REALLY HATE YOU!
WHIP
SCATTER
BEEEEEEEEEP
!!
!!
BEEEEP
YOU...
BEEEP
HATE ME?

ALL RIGHT, EVERY-ONE.
LET'S START WITH OUR VOCAL EXERCISES.

ONE!
TWO!
THREE!
GO!

AAAAAHHHHHHH~! ♪

AGGGHHHHHH!
GLANCE

MY! THIS IS THE FIRST TIME I'VE HAD TO ASK YOU TO BE LOUDER, WATANABE-SAN.
USUALLY, I HAVE TO DO THE OPPOSITE!

YOU NEED TO SING A LITTLE LOUDER TOO, YAMADA-SAN!
AH!
I'M SORRY.

I-I'M ON A DIET, SO I JUST DON'T HAVE THE STRENGTH IN MY CHEST RIGHT NOW...
OH?
ALL RIGHT, THEN.

REMEMBER, SINGING AND SPEAKING ARE NIGH ONE AND THE SAME IN A MUSICAL.
YOU NEED TO SPEAK AS IF YOU'RE SINGING, AND SING AS IF YOU'RE JUST SPEAKING.

WE DON'T WANT ANY DULL, HALF-HEARTED VOICES IN OUR MUSICALS! PROJECT, LOUD AND STRONG!
IMAGINE THAT YOU'RE TRYING TO SEND YOUR VOICE THROUGH TO THE OTHER SIDE OF A WALL.
OKAY, LET'S SPLIT INTO QUARTETS.
I KNOW!

YAMADA-SAN.
NARATA-SAN.
HOSHINO-SAN.
AND WATANABE-SAN.

OKAY!
TWO OF YOU, SING DO-RE-MI-FA-SO-FA-MI-RE. THE OTHER TWO, SING SO-FA-MI-RE-DO-RE-MI-FA.
AND GO!

GLANCE

HMPH!

AAAAAAHHHHH! ♪

AAGGHHHHHHH!

I WISH I COULD BLOCK THIS OUT.

FIRST-YEARS

I SWEAR!

ARE YOU EVEN *TRYING?*

YOU DO REALIZE THAT YOUR PERFORMANCE AFFECTS *OUR* PERFORMANCE, TOO?!
QUIT PLAYING AROUND!

I'M NOT PLAYING AROUND.
IT'S JUST... I FEEL SO WEAK BECAUSE OF MY DIET.

THEN HOW COME YOU JUST GET FATTER?

HOSHINO-SAN, DON'T BE MEAN TO HER!
I'M NOT BEING MEAN. I'M BEING *NICE.*
MEAN?
THIS ISN'T A SCHOOL WHERE WE ALL HOLD HANDS, SING SONGS, AND BE BESTIES.
ANYONE WHO CAME HERE EXPECTING THINGS TO BE EASY HAS A SCREW LOOSE.
YES. A STRONG WILL'S IMPORT-ANT.
SO'S TALENT.
EFFORT.
PAS-SION.
CONNEC-TIONS.

WHAT ARE YOU TRYING TO SAY?!
OH, NOTHING.
I'M JUST TALKING.
I'M GOING TO CLASS.
WOW, SUGIMOTO REALLY HIT HOSHINO-SAN'S SORE SPOT.
I HEARD SOME OF THE SECOND-YEARS TALKING ABOUT HOW THEY LET HOSHINO-SAN IN ONLY BECAUSE HER MOM AND GRANDMA WENT HERE.
CONNECTIONS AREN'T SOMETHING TO BE ASHAMED OF. THEY HELP YOU GET YOUR FOOT IN THE DOOR.
BUT IT TAKES MORE THAN THAT TO *TRULY* MAKE A MARK ON THE WORLD.

IF YOU HAVE CONNECTIONS AND CHANCES AND DON'T MAKE ANYTHING OF THEM, THEN YOU *REALLY* HAVE A SCREW LOOSE.
GLANCE
AS FOR THE REST OF US...
WE'LL JUST HAVE TO WORK HARDER TO ACHIEVE OUR DREAMS.

SUGIMOTO-SAN IS SO COOL!
EVERY-THING SHE SAYS IS JUST SO SMART!
WE'RE GOING, TOO!

WE DON'T HAVE CONNEC-TIONS EITHER, SO WE'LL WORK HARD! ♡

THAT'S RIGHT!

WHO SHOULD WE GO TALK TO?

NARATA-SAN'S A LOST CAUSE, SO HOSHINO-SAN!

GOOD CALL.

HEY, UH...
AI-CHAN?
Tanizawa
2 Albums, 13 Songs
Kajiura Chie
3 Albums, 27 Songs
Don Henry
1 Album, 8 Songs
I'M SORRY FOR SCREWING UP IN SINGING CLASS...
AND RUINING OUR QUARTET.
UMM, ALSO...
I WANTED TO ASK ABOUT THAT THING FROM EARLIER.

I DON'T KNOW WHY YOU GOT SO MAD AT ME.
COULD YOU...
TELL ME WHY YOU GOT ANGRY?
UMM ?
AI-CHAN?

SHK
IF I TELL YOU...
WILL YOU *FINALLY* LEAVE ME ALONE?

I FELT BAD...
FOR RUNNING OFF AND LEAVING YOU THERE LIKE THAT.
IT TOOK A LOT...
FOR ME TO RUN BACK THERE.
BUT WHEN I ARRIVED...
YOU WERE...!

YOU, AND TAICHI, AND THAT GUY...
HA HA HA!
HAI!
HAI!
HAI!
HAI!
WERE DANCING AROUND LIKE IDIOTS!
IT WAS SO STUPID!
AI-CHAN...
YOU...
ARE A BIG DUMMY.

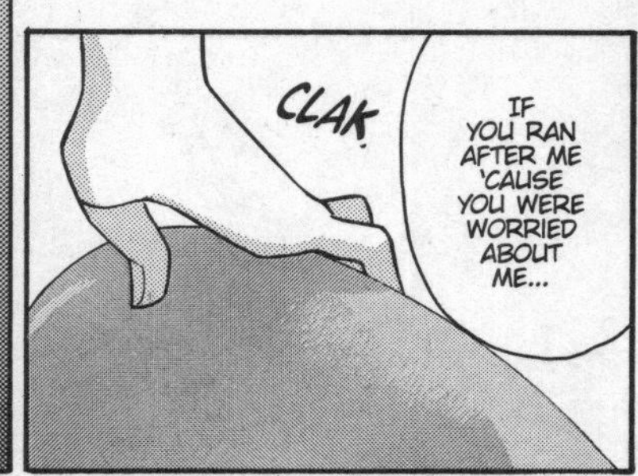

CLAK
IF YOU RAN AFTER ME 'CAUSE YOU WERE WORRIED ABOUT ME...

WELL!

GOOD! I'M GLAD!

BUT WHEN YOU SAW THAT I WAS OKAY...
THEN YOU SHOULD'VE BEEN RELIEVED, NOT... ANGRY.
......
WELL!
YOU CAN SAY WHAT-EVER YOU WANT!
JUST DON'T BOTHER ME ANYMORE, OKAY?
HMPH!
FINE!
THEN WE'RE THROUGH!
WE'RE THROUGH?
SHK
NOTHING'S THROUGH.
I TOLD YOU, WE AREN'T FRIENDS!

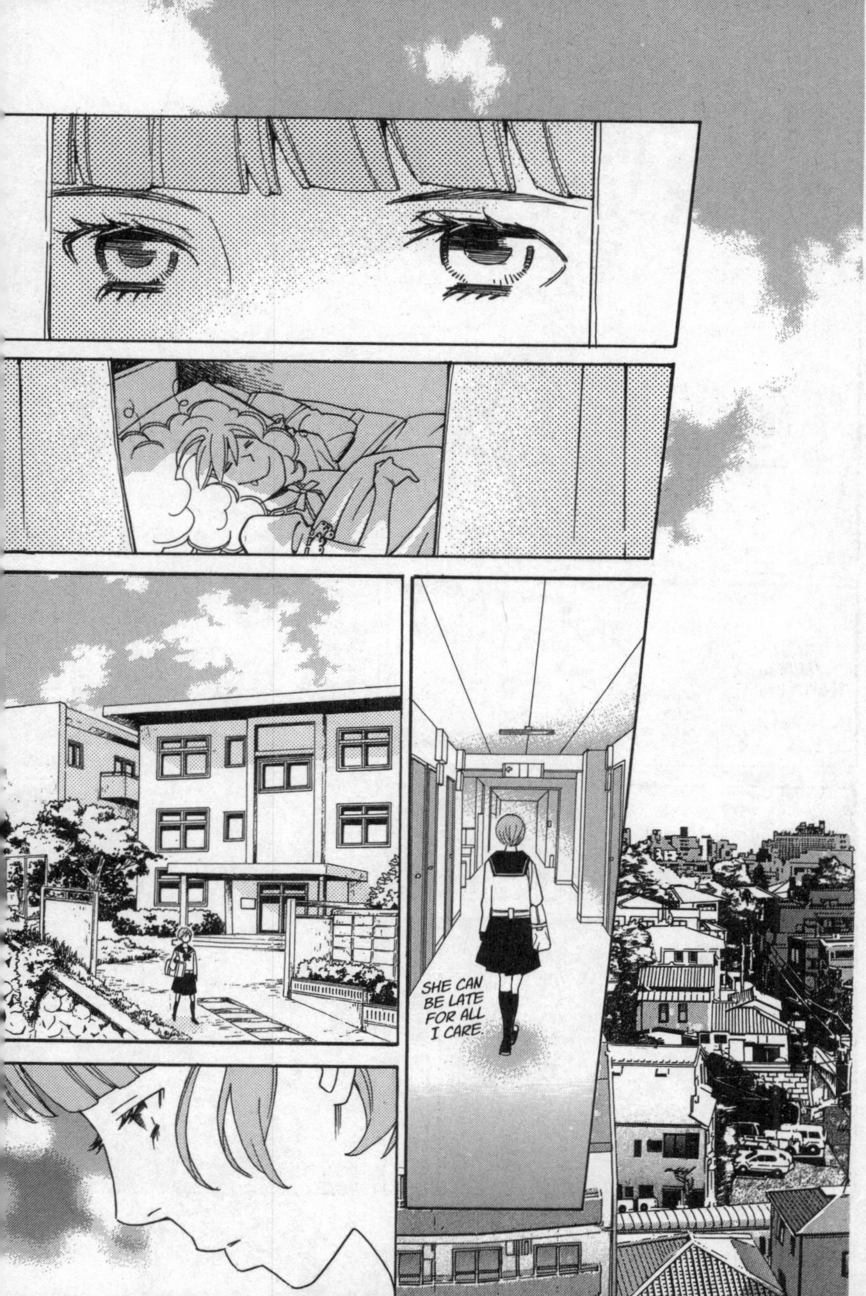
SHE CAN BE LATE FOR ALL I CARE.

I DON'T...
WANT TO GO TO CLASS.

COME ON, WATANABE-SAN!
WE HAVE FIVE MINUTES BEFORE WE'LL BE OFFICIALLY LATE!

RIGHT, SORRY!
PTOO!
YOU LOOK LIKE AN OLD-SCHOOL DELIN-QUENT.
WHERE'S AI-CHAN?

SHE WAS GONE WHEN I CAME TO WAKE YOU UP.

I CAN'T BELIEVE SHE'D GET BACK AT ME LIKE THIS.
HEH! NOT BAD.
YOU DO KNOW YOU JUST OVER-SLEPT, RIGHT?

Kouka School of Musical and Theatrical Arts

GOOD MORNING!

GOOD MORNING!

MORNING.

OH, RISA-SENPAI!

GOOD MORNING! WE'RE ALMOST DONE CLEANING!

MORNING.

YOU'RE AS ENERGETIC AS EVER, I SEE.

THAT'S NOT TRUE.

MY HEART IS A DEEP, DARK ABYSS THIS MORNING.

REALLY? DOESN'T SEEM LIKE IT!

HEY, SO...

NARATA-SAN DIDN'T COME TO CLEAN.
IS SHE SICK?

I DON'T KNOW. SHE WAS GONE WHEN I WOKE UP.

HMM. OKAY.
I'LL GO CHECK THE NURSE'S OFFICE, THEN.

GLANCE

?

NARATA-SAN? NO, I HAVEN'T SEEN HER.
MAYBE SHE CALLED IT QUITS AND WENT HOME?
NAH. NARATA-SAN MIGHT NOT WANT TO BE HERE, BUT SHE'S NOT AN IDIOT.
UNLIKE SOME-ONE WE KNOW.
OH? WHO?
WAIT, I HAVEN'T SEEN YAMADA-SAN, EITHER!
SHE WAS JUST HERE A SECOND AGO.
MAYBE SHE'S IN THE BATHROOM.
TOILET
BLEGH...
ゲボッ
BLEH!
ゲボッ
FLUUUSH
ゴポォ

WIPE

OH!

SORRY, NEVER MIND!

HEE HEE!
I TOTALLY FORGOT TO CHECK TWITTER!

I MADE SOMEONE I LIKE ANGRY AND SHE TOLD ME SHE HATED ME.

I DON'T UNDER-STAND.

SHE TOLD ME BEFORE WE'RE NOT EVEN FRIENDS, AND NOW SHE SAYS SHE HATES ME. IT'S PRETTY BAD.

NOBODY'S EVER TOLD ME THEY HATED ME. IT WAS A REAL SHOCK.

EVEN SO, I STILL...

Sarasa @sara3

@Jiraiya-bot Even so, I still won't start to hate her... because she has so many qualities I admire. I can't help but look up to her.

KOUZA-
BUROU!

YOU'VE BEEN IMPERSON-ATING ME ON TWITTER AGAIN!

COULD YOU JUST TELL ME YOUR PASSWORD ALREADY, AKIYA?
THIS GUY...

Don't feel like
take your time
Don't feel like you have to rush. You're still getting to know each other. Just take your time and keep at it.
But remember, you may not get what you want. Your feelings of friendship may only be one-sided in the end, and you'll just have to look on from afar.
But I think that's beautiful in its own way.
ONLY...
ONE-SIDED?
HUNH.

HEE HEE!

AKIYA-KUN IS SO POETIC!

WATA-NABE-SAN? LET'S GET TO CLASS.

I WISH SHE'D JUST QUIT SCHOOL.

HEY, ISN'T THAT A KOUKA UNIFORM?

YOU DON'T SEE 'EM AWAY FROM CAMPUS VERY OFTEN.

DUDE!

ISN'T THAT NARACCHI FROM JPX?!

WHOA, FOR REAL?!

HOLY SHIT, SHE'S HOT!

OH, MAN, I GOTTA POST A PIC, LIKE, NOW!

11

I'M GOOD AT FOLLOWING THE RULES.
I DO AS I'M TOLD, CARRY OUT MY DUTIES.
IT'S EASY.
I FORGOT MY PHONE.
I CAN'T EVEN LISTEN TO MUSIC.
I CAN SHUT OFF MY THOUGHTS AND FEELINGS THAT WAY.
FOUND NARAC-CHI!
KA-SNAP
POSTIN' A PIC!
FUNNILY ENOUGH, HAVING FREEDOM ONLY MAKES THINGS HARDER ON ME.

SECOND-YEARS
WHAT ARE YA DOING, TAKEI?
HMM?
OH, JUST THE MONTHLY SOCIAL MEDIA CHECK.
GOTTA MAKE SURE NOBODY'S POSTING ANYTHING WEIRD ABOUT OUR STUDENTS.
WOW, I DIDN'T KNOW THE SECOND-YEAR REP DID ALL THAT, TOO!
MUST BE ROUGH.
NOT REALLY. I JUST SEARCH FOR A FEW KEYWORDS.
I DON'T USUALLY FIND ANYTHING.
on.co.jp
KOUK
Kouka
Kouka School of Musical and Theatrical Ar
TAKA TAKA
HMM?
WHAT'S THIS?

WOW! THE R.A.'S BOX LUNCHES ARE AS INCREDIBLE AS ALWAYS!

LUNCH JUST TASTES BETTER WHEN SOMEONE MAKES IT FOR YOU!
YOU THINK SO?
IT'S JUST KIND OF BROWN.
IT'S NOT BAD, BUT IT'S NOT ESPECIALLY GOOD, YOU KNOW?

YAMADA-SAN, YOU FINISHED ALREADY?!
YOU EAT FAST!

HEE HEE! I DO?
CAREFUL! IF YOU EAT TOO QUICKLY, YOU'LL GET FAT!
TOTALLY!

I-I'M GOING TO THE BATH-ROOM.

SLIDE
OH!
WHOA!

SORRY TO STARTLE YOU, YAMADA-SAN.

WHAT'S UP, NARATA-SENSEI? CAN I HELP YOU WITH SOME-THING?
YEAH.

COULD YOU GET WATA-NABE-SAN FOR ME?

WE CAN'T...
FIND AI ANY-WHERE.

SHE DIDN'T GO TO SCHOOL, AND IT DOESN'T LOOK LIKE SHE WENT BACK TO HER ROOM. SHE'S NOT PICKING UP HER PHONE, EITHER.
DO YOU KNOW WHERE SHE MIGHT'VE GONE?

UMM, SHE MIGHT'VE GONE HOME IF SHE WASN'T FEELING WELL OR SOME-THING, BUT...DO YOU THINK SHE'S JUST SKIPPING CLASS?
NO. WHEN I WOKE UP, SHE'D ALREADY LEFT.
I HOPE SO.
HMM.

OKAY! THANKS FOR YOUR HELP.
I'LL HEAD OVER TO THE DORM.
SORRY TO BOTHER YOU DURING YOUR LUNCH BREAK.
AI WOULDN'T WANDER AROUND TOWN.
SHE STANDS OUT TOO MUCH.
AND SHE WOULDN'T WANT TO GIVE STRANGERS ANY REASON TO TALK TO HER...
SO, SHE WOULDN'T BREAK ANY RULES.

UM, SENSEI?
DO YOU THINK SHE WAS FEELING HOMESICK AND WENT BACK TO TOKYO?
NAH.
I DOUBT IT.

WATANABE-SAN?

COULD YOU COME WITH US FOR A MOMENT?

WHERE IS AI-CHAN?

DID SHE RUN AWAY BECAUSE I SAID WE WERE THROUGH?

NO WAY. SHE'D NEVER--

HEY!

ARE YOU LISTENING?

YES!

THIS IS YOU, RIGHT?

Kouka Fan♡ @Daisuki_KOOOKA!
Isn't that a Kouka student? Didn't know school rules were so lax nowadays. That's her BF, right?
pic.twitter.com/XXXXXX

WHOA! THAT'S ME, THAT'S *ME!*

AND THEY'VE BLACKED OUT MY EYES LIKE I'M SOME KIND OF **CRIMINAL!**

SO, YOU ADMIT IT?

I HEARD RUMORS THAT YOU HAD A BOYFRIEND, BUT WOW...

YOU'RE QUITE THE PAIR!

TEE HEE HEE!

KOUKA SCHOOL RULES STATE THAT ROMANTIC RELATIONSHIPS ARE ALLOWED, AS LONG AS THEY ARE NOT MADE PUBLIC.

FLAUNTING IT LIKE THIS AND GETTING YOUR PICTURE TAKEN REFLECTS BADLY ON THE SCHOOL AND OUR STUDENTS.

OH, BUT WE WEREN'T OUT THERE ALONE. NARATA-SENSEI WAS THERE WITH US, TOO.
NARATA-SENSEI? REALLY. I'LL HAVE TO TALK TO HIM, THEN.

OH DEAR!
IF THIS GETS OUT, THERE ARE DEFINITELY SOME SECOND-YEARS WHO'LL HAVE IT OUT FOR YOU.
BUT I BET YOUR LOVE IS WORTH MORE THAN THAT, HUH?

HE'S NOT MY BOYFRIEND, THOUGH.
HE'S...

AI-CHAN'S BIGGEST FAN.
A MAN WHO LOVES AI-CHAN...
A KIND, CARING GUY.

OH!

ガタ
BLAM
SORRY, SENPAI! I JUST REMEM-BERED SOMETHING SUPER IMPORTANT I GOTTA DO!
CAN WE CONTINUE THIS...
MAYBE SOMETIME TONIGHT ?!
DING-A-LING DING-A-LING-LING

HELLO?
HELLO? IS THIS OTAKU-SAN?
OTAKU-SAN? I THINK YOU HAVE THE WRONG NUMBER.

YOU'RE CREEPY GROSS OTAKU-SAN, RIGHT?

UHHHHH...

YES?

THAT'S ME...

*Vending machines text: Coca-Cola

YES. I'M STILL IN KOBE. SORRY.
I WANTED TO SEE CHINATOWN WHILE I WAS HERE.
HUH?
NARACCHI'S IN TROUBLE?!

*Sign: Choanmon Gate

I'M BORED ...
OF THE OCEAN.
I'VE NEVER SKIPPED SCHOOL BEFORE, SO I'M NOT SURE WHAT TO DO NOW.
MAYBE I'LL JUST HEAD BACK TO THE DORM.

I WONDER IF ANYONE'S NOTICED I'M MISSING.
ARE THEY EVEN WORRIED ABOUT ME?

HEY, 'SCUSE ME!
I'M KINDA LOST, AND WAS HOPING YOU COULD HELP.

CAN YA SHOW ME HOW TO GET TO THE OCEAN?!
GLOM
JUST KIDDING!
SHUDDERR
WHOA, NO *WAAAAY!* AREN'T YOU NARAC-CHI?!
WHOA, DUDE, YEAH WAY! IT'S TOTALLY HER!
OH MAN!
I'M A TOTAL NARACCHI STAN!
SHIT, ME TOO! I *LOOOOVE* HOW CUTE HER LITTLE FACE IS!
THAT KOMOMO BITCH IS POPULAR BUT SHE'S A TOTAL BUTTERFACE, DON'T YA THINK?
DUDE, I'M SO FRICKIN' PUMPED RIGHT NOW!
OH, HEY, CAN I GET A SELFIE WITH YA? YEAH?
STOP.

STOP IT!
WHY IS IT SO HARD...
LET GO!
LEAVE ME ALONE!
TO LIVE IN THIS WORLD?
HUH?
STOP IT!
NO...
PLEASE!
JUST STOP...
THAT'S NOT IT.

WHY DID I...
END UP LIKE THIS?
PLEASE, STOP ...
WHAT? SHEESH. CALM DOWN.
WE JUST ASKED FOR A PICTURE.
YOU TWO!
QUIT IT!

GET YOUR HANDS ...!
OFF HER !
HRAAH!
TMP TMP TMP TMP TMP TMP TMP
CRACK

OWW! WHAT'S YOUR DAMAGE, MAN?!
SHE OBVI-OUSLY WANTS YOU TO GO AWAY!

SO TAKE YOUR HANDS OFF HER!!
WHAT ?!

WHO ARE YOU, HER STALK-ER?
OR JUST CAPTAIN SAVE A HO?

I'M NOT SCARED! I'M NOT SCARED OF YOU OR YOU!

TRYIN' TO BE SHINJI NOW? GOD, YOU'RE ANNOYING!
WHAP
I MUS --
GAH!
I MUSTN'T RUN AWAY! I MUSTN'T RUN AWAY! I MUSTN'T RUN AWAY!

OH, GOD, I'M SCAR-ED!
WHAT DO I DO?
WHAT DO I DO?!
WHOA DUDE!
STARE

OHHHH, WOW! YOU FOUND HER!

AI-
CHAN!

AI!
OUR FRIENDSHIP IS OVER, AI-CHAN.
BUT I'LL HELP YOU.
JUST THIS ONCE, OKAY?
HAAH!
YOU OKAY, AI?
EEEEEEEK!!

HEEEE-EELP! THESE GUYS WON'T LEAVE ME ALOOO-OONE!
WHA ?!
SHE'S SO LOUD!

HEEEELP!
AND SHE'S HUGE!
YOU SURE SHE'S A CHICK?!

THESE GUYS ARE HARASSING TWO SWEET, INNOCENT GIRLS!
SHE INCLUDED HERSELF!
YEESH!

MURMUR

WE WEREN'T FORCING HER!
YEAH! SHE FREAKED OUT OVER NOTHING!

HMPH! WEAK-LINGS.

YOU HEARD HER! YOU'RE COMING TO THE STATION WITH ME!
WAIT! THAT'S THE WRONG GUY!

HUH? YOU'RE A TEACHER AT KOUKA?
WOW!

HOW...
DID YOU KNOW I WAS HERE?

OTAKU-SAN.
HE CAME LOOKING FOR YOU HERE.
I GOT HIS CONTACT DETAILS WHEN WE MET BEFORE.

The ocean! She's gotta be near the ocean!
The ocean?
That's right!
In the October 2012 MyoJaw, and the March 2013 POCO Magazine, and the JPX official newsletter...

Naracchi said that the ocean makes her feel calm!

Okay, but that doesn't really narrow it down.

I'll take a look at social media, then!

カチャ KER-CHACK

She's pretty *and* famous, so I bet I can find where she is just by seeing who's mentioned her!

Okay! I'll tell Narata-sensei that, too.

Right!

I gotta...

I gotta...

find her, and fast!

BAAAAAM!

⟨ENTER⟩

WATA-NABE-SAN, CAN WE TALK TO YOU FOR A SEC?
JUST EXPLAIN THE SITUATION TO HIM.
SHF
SNRK

AH!
HUH?

YOU'RE BLEED-ING.
TAKE THIS.

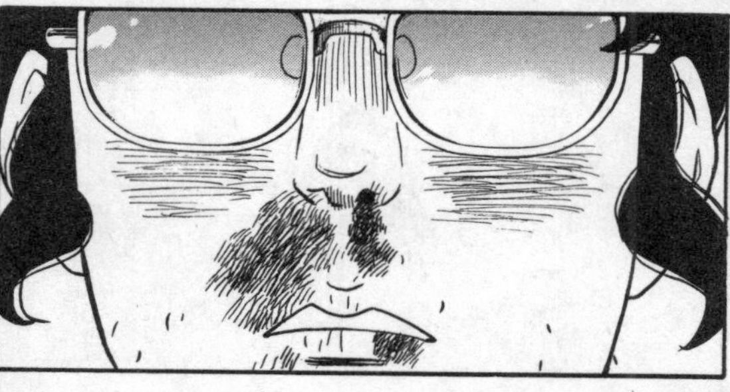

SLIP

PLAP

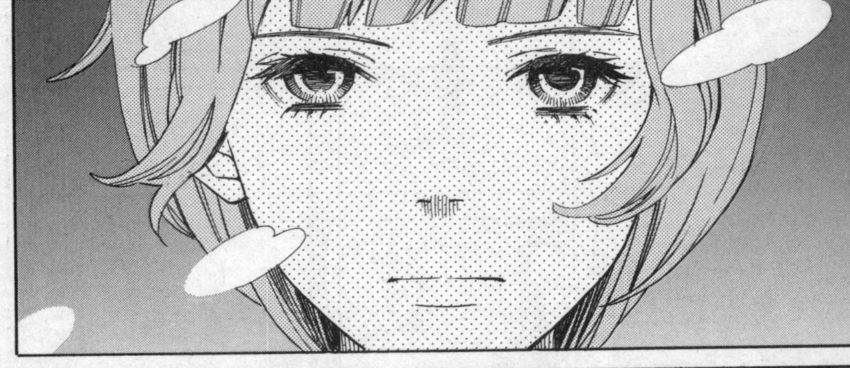

GLOOM
IT'S NOT WHAT YOU THINK.
I'M REALLY SORRY.
THANK YOU.
I'M REALLY...
TRYING MY BEST RIGHT NOW.
I... NO, WE...
WE ONLY WANTED TO SEE YOU SMILE, NARACCHI.
IT'S OKAY! REALLY!
PLEASE, DON'T CRY.
I DON'T THINK I'LL EVER SEE YOU UP CLOSE LIKE THIS AGAIN...
SO PLEASE LET ME KEEP THIS HANDKER-CHIEF OF YOURS.
I'M SORRY FOR SCARING YOU BEFORE.

ONE DAY, I'LL COME SEE YOU PERFORM ON THE BIG KOUKA STAGE!
WHEN THAT DAY COMES, I HOPE I'LL SEE YOUR SMILE ONCE MORE.
FARE-WELL!
AND THANK YOU.
UNTIL...
WE MEET AGAIN!
BY THE TIME WE FINISHED UP WITH THE POLICEMAN...
THE SUN WAS STARTING TO SET.
CREEPY OTAKU-SAN WAS A NICE GUY.
I FOUND OUT HIS REAL NAME WAS KITAOUJI MIKIYA.
WHAT A COOL NAME!

I WAS EXHAUSTED MENTALLY AND PHYSICALLY, WHICH MADE ME BLURT OUT SOMETHING I SHOULDN'T HAVE.
HEY.
IF THERE'S SOME-THING I WANT TO FORGET ABOUT, BUT CAN'T...
WHAT SHOULD I DO ABOUT IT?
NOT SURPRISED.
ANYBODY WOULD BE WEIRDED OUT BY A RANDOM QUESTION LIKE THAT.
WELL...
I'M STILL ONLY FIFTEEN.
THERE'S A LOT I HAVE TO LEARN ABOUT THE WORLD.

BUT EVEN IF YOU CAN'T FORGET SOMETHING HAPPENED...

YOU CAN STILL MAKE NEW MEMORIES BY HAVING FUN AND POURING YOUR HEART INTO THE THINGS YOU LOVE.

JUST KEEP OVERWRITING THE BAD MEMORIES WITH LOTS OF GOOD ONES...

AND EVENTUALLY, THE BAD WILL FADE AWAY.

I DIDN'T SEE HER EXPRESSION WHEN SHE SAID THAT.

I THINK THAT MIGHT HELP.

I WAS WALKING BEHIND HER.

WHEN WE GOT BACK TO SCHOOL, THE SECOND-YEARS WERE WAITING FOR US.

FOR THE FOLLOWING WEEK, WATANABE SARASA AND I HAD OUR MORNING CLEANING HOURS DOUBLED.

12

NOW, LADIES.
YOU'RE STUDENTS AT THE KOUKA SCHOOL OF MUSICAL AND THEATRICAL ARTS!
THAT MEANS THAT AS LONG AS YOU KEEP YOUR CHIN UP AND PERSEVERE, YOU'LL END UP ON STAGE WITH THE KOUKA TROUPE ONE DAY.
WE LIVE IN A GLORIOUS AGE OF INFORMATION! YOU CAN FIND ALL SORTS OF INFORMATION ONLINE--BOTH TRUE AND UNTRUE.
DROOP
PROTECT YOUR FUTURE CAREER BY LIVING A LIFE OF DISCIPLINE AND BEAUTY.

WHAT WAS ALL *THAT* ABOUT?
YOU DIDN'T HEAR? SOMEONE POSTED A PICTURE OF THAT "OSCAR" GIRL AND SOME DUDE.
WHAT?! NO WAY!

WELL, *I* HEARD IT GOT OUT THAT NARACCHI WAS SKIPPING CLASS.
YIKES. NOT A GOOD LOOK FOR OUR HUN-DREDTH ANNIVER-SARY.

HEY.

THE THING WITH WATA-NABE-SAN...

WAS ENTIRELY MY FAULT.

SHE HAD NOTHING TO DO WITH IT.
I'M SORRY FOR CAUSING SUCH A RUCKUS.
CLAP CLAP CLAP CLAP CLAP
AWW! YOU'RE SO KIND, NARATA-SAN!
LOOK AT YOU, TRYING TO TAKE THE BLAME!
IT'S ALL RIGHT.
SHE GOT A WARNING, BUT I KNOW IT'S JUST A MISUNDER-STANDING.

NEXT TIME YOU'RE IN TROUBLE, TELL ME!
PLEASE? PROM-ISE?
......

WATA-NABE-SAN! AT LEAST WAKE UP TO WALK!

OH!

HEY, HIJIRI. IT WAS YOU, WASN'T IT?

WHAT DO YOU MEAN, RISA?
I MEAN *YOU* WERE THE ONE WHO CAUSED ALL THE "RUCKUS."

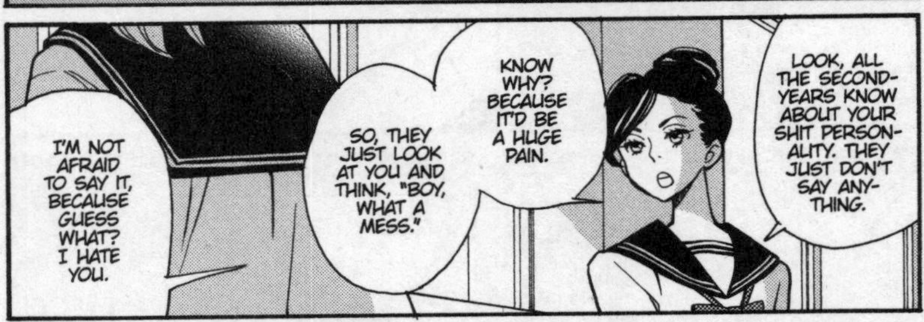
LOOK, ALL THE SECOND-YEARS KNOW ABOUT YOUR SHIT PERSONALITY. THEY JUST DON'T SAY ANYTHING.
KNOW WHY? BECAUSE IT'D BE A HUGE PAIN.
SO, THEY JUST LOOK AT YOU AND THINK, "BOY, WHAT A MESS."
I'M NOT AFRAID TO SAY IT, BECAUSE GUESS WHAT? I HATE YOU.

AND NOW YOU'VE REALLY CROSSED THE LINE!

I DON'T KNOW WHAT YOU'RE TALKING ABOUT.

BUT NOW I KNOW *FOR SURE* YOU DON'T LIKE ME.
THAT'S TOO BAD!

SO? WHAT HAP-PENED?
IT WAS ONE BIG MISUNDER-STANDING!
SO THAT GUY WASN'T YOUR BOYFRIEND, WATANABE-SAN?
STRETCH
NO WAY!
Yeah, her BF's a Twitter bot.
A frog Twitter bot.
A 2D anime husband.
DID YOU LOSE WEIGHT, YAMADA-SAN?
YOU THINK SO?!
I KNOW THE BASICS ARE IMPORTANT, BUT IT'S SO BORING JUST DOING THE BASICS EVERY DAY!
I WISH WE COULD DO SOME-THING SUPER FLOWERY AND CRAZY SOMETIMES!
YAY! MY DIET'S FINALLY WORK-ING!
BING
BONG
BENG
BONG
OH, THAT'S THE BELL!
SOME-THING WAY MORE KOUKA!

*Each troupe has their own pose.

I'VE BEEN MEANING TO ASK...

WHAT KOUKA SHOWS DO YOU LIKE BESIDES *THE ROSE OF VERSAILLES?*

UMM, UHH...
TO TELL YOU THE TRUTH, I DON'T KNOW MANY OTHERS...

WHAT?! ARE YOU SERIOUS?!
THERE ARE SO MANY OTHER FAMOUS SHOWS!
YOU CAN GET THE KOUKA CHANNEL ON CABLE, FOR GOD'S SAKE!
MY GRANDPA ALWAYS HAD THE REMOTE, SO WE WATCHED MOSTLY PERIOD PIECES...
OH, BUT I HAD *RoV* ON VHS AND WATCHED THAT, LIKE, A MILLION TIMES!
ROV
VHS?!
YOU STILL USED A VCR?!
LOOK! OUR POOR CLASS REP IS TOTALLY DEPRESSED BECAUSE OF YOU, WATANABE-SAN!
SUGIMOTO-SAN LOVES THE WINTER TROUPE MORE THAN ANYTHING!

UMM? SUGI-MOTO-SAN?
THIS ...
THIS IS PERFECT, WATANABE-SAN!
THIS AFTERNOON, WE'RE GOING TO SEE A SHOW!
YOU'LL SEE THAT THERE ARE SHOWS OUT THERE THAT ARE JUST AS AMAZING AS RoV!
BAM
Don't sulk when you can share!!
WE'RE GONNA SEE A SHOW?!
YES! LOTS OF SHOWS THROUGH-OUT THE YEAR!
KOUKA THEATER
KOUKA
SEEING REAL, LIVE KOUKA SHOWS...
IS AN IMPORTANT PART OF OUR EDUCATION!

ROMEO AND JULIET
LAST DANCE
OH, WOW!
THIS IS *JUST* LIKE THE TOKYO THEATER I WENT TO WHEN I WAS LITTLE!
KEEP YOUR VOICE DOWN!
ROMEO AND JULIET
LAST DANCE
SEE HOW IT SAYS "LAST" THERE?
WHEN YOU SEE THE WORDS "LAST" OR "GOODBYE" IN THE SUB-TITLE OF SHOWS...
IT MEANS IT'S THE LAST PERFORMANCE FOR THE STAR OF THE SHOW.

THIS WILL BE THE FINAL KOUKA PERFORMANCE FOR THE TOP STAR OF THE WINTER TROUPE, KAZAHANA SOU.
WOW! YOU MUST BE A BIG FAN, SUGIMOTO-SAN!
DON'T CRY!

WATANA--
WHOA, IT'S THE JPX GIRL!

HEY, DON'T BOTHER HER, SEI!

OH, RIGHT.

SORRY.

GOOD MORNING!

YOU THE NEW FIRST-YEARS? YOU'RE SO CUTE!
HOW'S THE PHANTOM DOING?

ANDOU-SENSEI'S DOING WELL!
PHANTOM?

TELL HIM I SAID HI.

THAT'S THE SECOND BIGGEST STAR OF THE WINTER TROUPE, SATOMI SEI-SAN!
IF SHE'S NUMBER TWO, WHY IS SHE NOT PERFORMING TODAY?

SEI-SAMA PERFORMED AS TYBALT IN THE FIRST RUN OF THE PERFORMANCES.
MAYBE SHE'LL PLAY ROMEO AND BECOME THE WINTER TROUPE'S NEW BIGGEST STAR.
THEIR NEW BIGGEST STAR?!
UM, WATANABE-SAN?
I'VE--
WHOA!
BRRRRMMM
IT'S STARTING!
LADIES AND GENTLEMEN, THANK YOU FOR COMING TO THE KOUKA THEATER TODAY.
I AM KAZAHANA SOU OF THE WINTER TROUPE.
THE WINTER TROUPE IS PROUD TO PRESENT WILLIAM SHAKESPEARE'S *ROMEO AND JULIET.*
TAICHI...

"I'VE NEVER FOUGHT WITH SOMEONE BEFORE.
"I THINK IT'S STUPID TO LET YOUR EMOTIONS GET THE BETTER OF YOU AND LASH OUT AT ANOTHER PERSON. IT'S BETTER TO JUST GET ALONG, RIGHT?
"THAT'S HOW I'VE GOTTEN BY ALL THESE YEARS, AND HOW I WANTED TO KEEP LIVING, TOO, BUT...
"WHAT SHOULD I DO, TAICHI?
"HEY, TAICHI?

"I DON'T KNOW HOW...
"TO MAKE UP WITH HER."
THE FEUD BETWEEN THE MONTAGUES AND THE CAPULETS...
MAY GO ON FOREVER.
AH!
NOW LISTEN, AND LISTEN WELL.
THESE HOUSES MAY NEVER UNDER-STAND ONE ANOTHER, 'TIS TRUE.

WOW!

KOUKA THEATER
KOUKA

SPARKLE
SPARKLE
GLOW
GLOW

THAT WAS AMAZING!
THE THEME SONG FROM THAT SHOW IS SUPER FAMOUS!
I'VE NEVER SEEN SUCH A FANTASTIC, SPARKLING SHOW!

YES.
IT WAS BEAUTIFUL.
SURPRISINGLY SO.
IN TWO YEARS...
WE'LL BE UP THERE!
I'M SO EXCITED!
I FEEL LIKE PAZU WHEN HE FIRST SPOTS LAPUTA IN THE SKY!
O, HOW MY HEART RACES!
I WOULD FLY O'ER THESE WALLS...
WITH THESE WINGS OF LOVE FOR YOU!

THOSE ARE ROMEO'S LINES.
INDEED, LET ME SWEAR THIS LOVE TO YOU...
UPON THE PALE MOON ABOVE!
WITH WHAT WORDS SHOULD I PROFESS MY DEEPEST LOVE FOR YOU?
HUH? WHAT?
WATA-NABE-SAN HASN'T SEEN THE SHOW BEFORE TODAY, RIGHT?
DID SHE MEMO-RIZE IT AL-READY?
LOOK! UPON THE PITCH-BLACK CURTAIN OF NIGHT...
SPARKLE A THOUSAND BRILLIANT STARS!!

EVERY-
ONE...
MUST
HAVE
NOTICED
IT IN
THAT
MOMENT.
WITHOUT
THINK-
ING...
THEY
LOOKED
UP TO
THE
SKY.
AND
THERE...
THEY
SAW
THEM-
SELVES.

THERE, AMONGST THE COUNT-LESS STARS SHINING ABOVE...

THE STAR THAT SHONE THE BRIGHT-EST...
FROM THE HIGHEST POINT IN THE SKY.
I SAW A STAR.
THAT STAR...

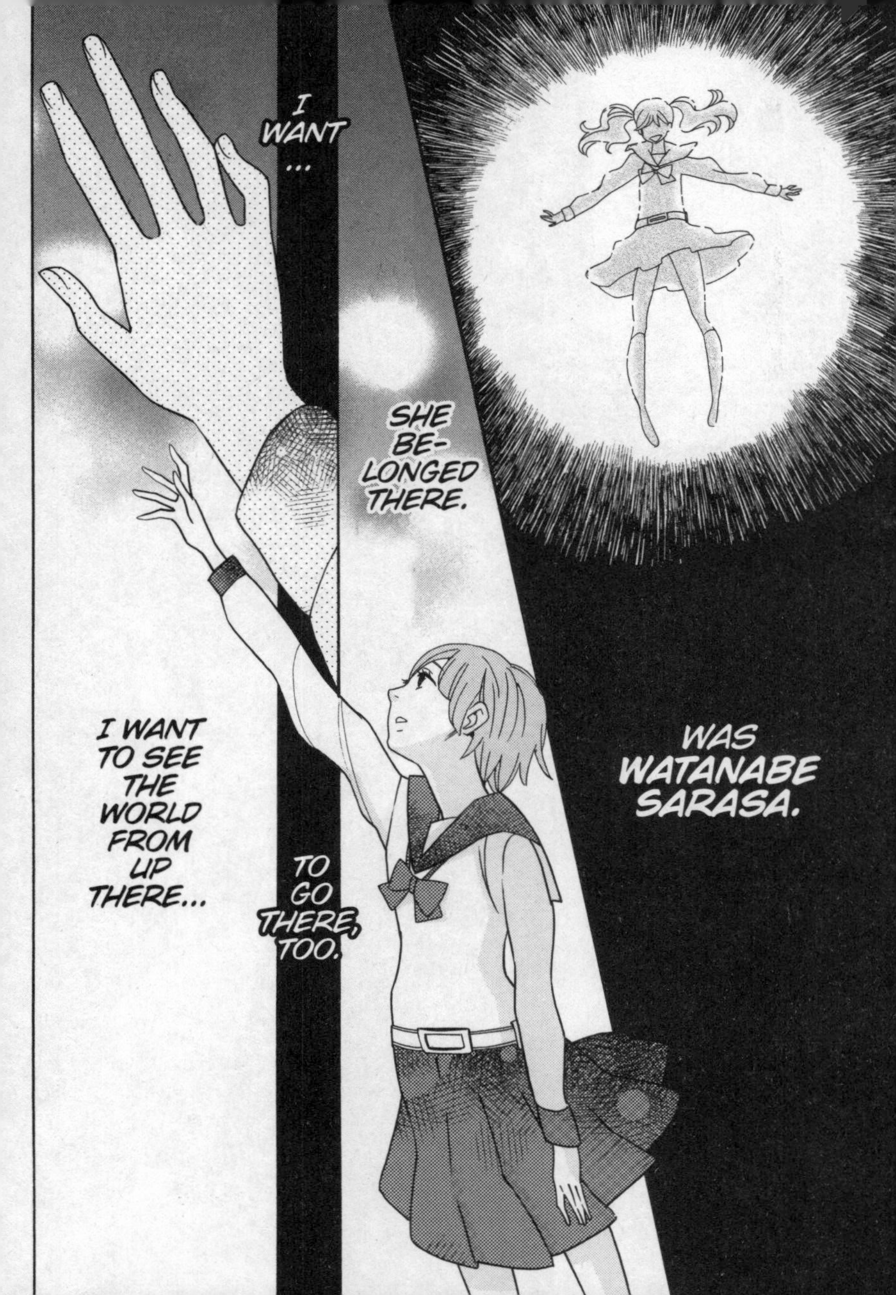
WAS WATANABE SARASA.
SHE BE-LONGED THERE.
I WANT ...
TO GO THERE, TOO.
I WANT TO SEE THE WORLD FROM UP THERE...

FROM WHERE SHE IS!

AH!

SHE DIDN'T ...

HAVE TO ACT SO STARTLED.

SHEESH!

"DON'T THINK TOO HARD ABOUT WHAT YOU WANT HER TO THINK, OR WHAT YOU SHOULD SAY TO FEEL BETTER.

"WORK UP YOUR COURAGE, AND JUST TELL HER, STRAIGHT OUT.

"JUST PUT YOUR FEELINGS INTO WORDS OF LOVE AND SPEAK THEM, HONEST AND TRUE."

UM, I...
UH!
I...
I WANT TO BE FRIENDS WITH YOU, WATANABE-SAN!

I'M SO GLAD!
I THOUGHT MY FEELINGS WOULD BE ONE-SIDED FOREVER!
Flower Road
YOU KNOW SOME-THING?
EVER SINCE THE MOMENT I MET YOU, AI-CHAN...

I REALLY, REALLY, REALLY...

WANTED TO BE YOUR FRIEND!

THAT...

MAKES ME HAPPY.
THANK YOU.

KAGEKI SHOJO!!

The Curtain Rises

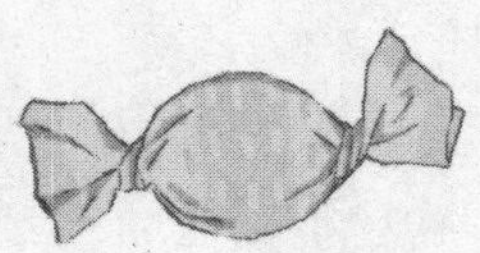

KAGEKI SHOJO!!

The Curtain Rises

Chapter 13

"I WANNA BE SUKE-ROKU! I'M GONNA BE SUKE-ROKU AND STAMP MY FEET ON THE FLOOR, AND WALK DOWN THE HANAMA-CHI*!"
"HA HA HA! SOUNDS GOOD. CAN'T WAIT TO SEE IT!"

*A hanamachi is part of the kabuki stage. It is a runway that extends out into the audience.

13

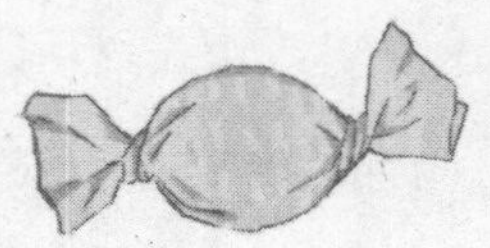

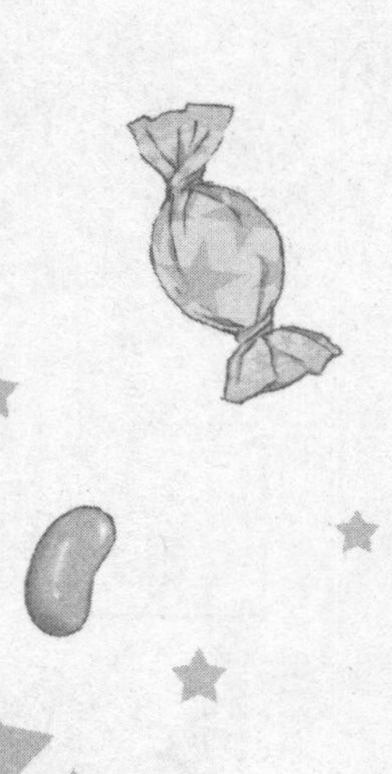

KAGEKI SHOJO!!

The Curtain Rises

JULY.
OUR UNIFORMS CHANGED TO THEIR SUMMER VER-SIONS.
AND BEFORE I KNEW IT...
THE DISTANCE BETWEEN EVERYONE GREW SMALLER.
SOON, WE WERE CALLING EACH OTHER BY GIVEN NAMES OR NICK-NAMES.
OH, MAN, I'M SOOOO HUNGRY!
YO, SARASA, SCOOT OVER!
WHERE'D THE SAWADA TWINS GO?
MAKE ROOM FOR SAWA!
OVER HERE!

SA... WATANABE-SAN?
WHAT'S UP, AI-CHAN?
I'M GONNA GO TO THE BATH-ROOM.
OKAY! DON'T FALL IN!
WEIRD.
I THOUGHT GIRLS **LIKED** TO GO TO THE BATHROOM TOGETHER.
IS THAT NOT TRUE?
AI-CHAN!
AI-CHAN, HOLD UP!

YOU'RE COMING TO THE BATHROOM WITH ME?!

?

NO?

THEY POSTED OUR MIDTERM GRADES!

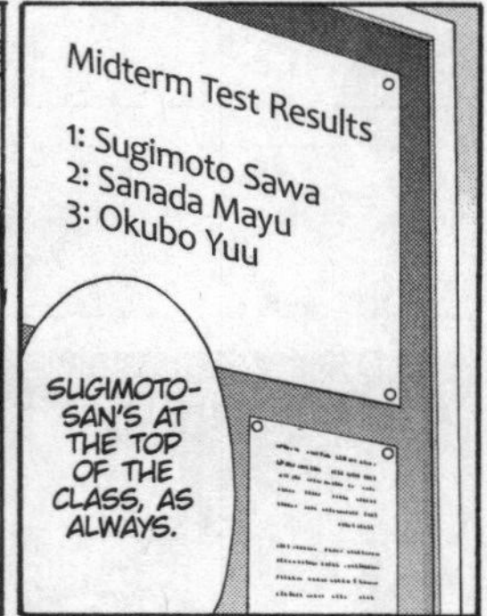

Midterm Test Results
1: Sugimoto Sawa
2: Sanada Mayu
3: Okubo Yuu
SUGIMOTO-SAN'S AT THE TOP OF THE CLASS, AS ALWAYS.

SHE SURE IS SMART!

WHERE AM I?!

22: Harada Maiko
23: Kimura Keiko
24: Narata Ai
25: Matsumoto Moe
Ooshima Tomoharu
I'M 24TH.
OOOH!
YES! I'M KILLING IT!
I WENT FROM FORTY TO THIRTY-NINE!
8: Nakai Shun
39: Watanabe Sarasa
40: Yamada Ayako
......
CON-GRATS.

39: Watanabe Sarasa
40: Yamada Ayako
End of list
OH, NO.
I'VE FALLEN ALL THE WAY TO THE BOTTOM.
COME NOW, YAMADA-SAN! I CAN'T HEAR YOU AT ALL!
OH.
SORRY.

ARE YOU FEELING SICK?
SLEEPING ALL RIGHT? EATING ENOUGH?
YOU LOOK A LITTLE PALE...
IT'S OKAY. I'M FINE.

FIRST THEY TELL ME TO LOSE WEIGHT, NOW THEY WANT ME TO EAT?
TENOR
PICK ONE ALREADY.

I'M SO HUNGRY.

HOW'D I EVEN GET INTO THIS SCHOOL, ANYWAY?

I SAW MY FIRST KOUKA PERFORMANCE WHEN I WAS EIGHT.

I WAS BLOWN AWAY. IT WAS LIKE A FAIRY TALE COME TO LIFE.

AFTER THAT, I WENT TO SEE A KOUKA PERFORMANCE...

EVERY YEAR ON MY BIRTHDAY.

WHEN I WENT TO KARAOKE, I'D ONLY SING KOUKA SONGS.
What is that?
No clue.
WHEN I STARTED MIDDLE SCHOOL, I WANTED TO LEARN HOW TO DANCE, SO I STARTED TAKING BALLET LESSONS.
THEN...
What?!
You want to go to Kouka?!
Oh, no, I just wanna take the test.
You're a first-year in high school, right? Are you even old enough to take the test?
Y-yeah.
WTF?! A higher percentage of appli-cants got into Tokyo U than Kouka last year?!
That's crazy!
Aha...
Yeah, I know my chances are low.
I just wanted to try.

Hmmm. You graduate in two years, so it'd be the same as just going to high school.
Well, shoot. Why not try?
You're right.
......
Huh?!
Well?! Why not?!
You've always loved singing and dancing, Ayako!
I'm just gonna try to find a job since I dunno what I want to do.
But you know what you wanna do, so it's a waste not to go after it.
I bet mom and dad would be cool with it.
If you happen to get in, well, I'll help pay your tuition, too.

SO NOW WHAT?

BUT I CAN'T KEEP UP WITH CLASSES.

I CAN'T JUST TELL THEM I WANT TO QUIT.

AND I'M NOT AS PRETTY AS EVERYONE ELSE.

FLUUUUUSH
RUSTLE

SNACK PIE

RIP

サク

CRUNCH

MUNCH

MUNCH

MUNCH

MUNCH

MUNCH

HUH? WHERE'D YOU GO, AI-CHAN?

BATH-ROOM.
YOU KNOW.
BY MY-SELF.
YOU GOTTA GET CHANGED! IT'S ALMOST TIME!

AH!
SHOOT! WE'RE DOING JAPANESE DANCE TODAY!

FWIP
FWIP
FWIP
FWIP
FWIP
WHOA! IMPRESSIVE QUICK CHANGE, AI-CHAN!

WE HAD TO DO THEM A LOT IN JPX.
UH, AI-CHAN? YOU'RE DOING THAT BACK-WARDS.
ONLY CORPSES WEAR IT LIKE THAT.

WE HAVE TO HURRY, SO I'LL HELP YOU FINISH UP.

SA--
WATANABE-SAN, YOU'RE REALLY FAST WHEN IT COMES TO KIMONOS.
THAT'S COOL.
IT'S LIKE WE'RE FRIENDS.
MY GRANDMA TAUGHT ME WHEN I WAS LITTLE.
BLUSH
THANKS, SA... WATANABE-SAN.
YOU'RE WELCOME!
HURRY UP, YOU TWO!
NOW, GIRLS, I KNOW I'VE SAID THIS A HUNDRED TIMES.
BUT TRADITIONAL JAPANESE DANCE IS THE CRYSTALLIZATION OF YEARS OF JAPANESE HISTORY.

THERE ARE VARYING TRADITIONS OF JAPANESE DANCE: *MAI*, A DELICATE STYLE THAT EVOLVED FROM NOH THEATER.
AND *ODORI*, WHICH COMES TO US FROM THE WORLD OF KABUKI.
PERFORMANCES ARE MADE UP OF *FURI*, OR DANCE MOVES.
YOU MUST ALSO UNDERSTAND THE **MEANING** OF THE SONG YOU ARE DANCING TO.

THERE ARE PLENTY OF KOUKA SHOWS THAT ARE BASED ON JAPANESE HISTORY OR TRADITIONS, SO YOU'LL USE THIS IN YOUR FUTURE!
THAT'S VERY GOOD!
HAVE YOU DONE TRADITIONAL DANCE BEFORE, WATANABE-SAN?
OH, YES!
NOTHING SERIOUS, THOUGH. I JUST DID IT AS A HOBBY UNTIL I WAS SIX.
I HAVEN'T DONE IT AT ALL SINCE THEN.
?!
SHE'S ACTUALLY BEING HUMBLE ABOUT IT?!

MAY I ASK WHO WAS YOUR TEACHER?

I LEARNED AT THE SHIRAKAWA SCHOOL OF DANCE.
MY TEACHER WAS SHIRAKAWA TOMOE.

EH?!

HO
JiraiyaBot @jiraiya-b
@sara3 He got a litt
mad at me lol
JiraiyaBot @jir
Just wanted to
JiraiyaBot
@sara3

I SEE!
IS THAT SO?

KIRISHIMA-SENSEI!

I'M NOT VERY GOOD AT PUTTING ON KIMONOS, SO, UH...
DO YOU KNOW ANY GOOD BOOKS I COULD READ?

I HAVE TO SAY, NARATA-SAN...

YOU'VE ALWAYS TAKEN CLASS SERIOUSLY, BUT I CAN TELL THAT YOU'VE BEEN A LOT MORE MOTIVATED LATELY.

I THINK THAT'S GREAT!

YOUR TEXTBOOK HAS A SECTION ON PROPER DRESSING TECHNIQUES.

SHOOT!

BUT I CAN LEND YOU ANOTHER BOOK IF YOU LIKE!

OH HO HO!

IT WAS IN THE TEXT-BOOK? DAMMIT.

ONE MORE THING... I'M CURIOUS ABOUT SHIRAKAWA TOMOE.

JAPANESE DANCE TRADI-TIONS CAN BE TRACED BACK TO EITHER A FAMOUS KABUKI CHOREO-GRAPHER...

OR A FAMOUS KABUKI ACTOR.

THE SHIRAKAWA SCHOOL IS ONE OF THE SIX MAIN SCHOOLS OF JAPANESE DANCE...

AND THE CURRENT HEAD OF THAT FAMILY IS SHIRAKAWA KAOU, FIFTEENTH OF HIS NAME.

HOWEVER, THE FAMILY MEMBER WHO'S CURRENTLY LEADING THEIR FAMILY DANCE TRADITION IS SHIRAKAWA TOMOE.
WATANABE-SAN WAS TAUGHT BY ONE OF THE BEST.
I NOTICED IT BACK WHEN THE JSDF CAME FOR THEIR DRILL, TO TELL THE TRUTH!
THE KABUKI PLAY.
MIIIN
I GUESS MY GUT INSTINCT WAS RIGHT!
MIIIIIN
MIIIN

IT'S SO QUIET WHEN THE SECOND-YEARS ARE GONE!
I KNOW! I DON'T EVEN HAVE TO WAIT TO DO LAUNDRY!

MIIIN
MIIIN
YOU OKAY?
MIIIN
MIIIN
OH?
OH! I KNOW IT LOOKS BAD, BUT I'M OKAY!
I JUST *REALLY* DON'T LIKE THE SOUND OF CICADAS.
PLUS, BECAUSE I'M SO TALL, I'M CLOSER TO THE SUN AND END UP CATCHING MORE UV RAYS.
IS THAT A THING?

HEY, OUR FAMILY JUST SENT US A WHOLE BUNCH OF *MONAKA* CAKES!
WANT SOME?
WHOA, NICE!
SARASA, NARACCHI, COME JOIN US!
I WANT GREEN TEA FLAVOR.
I'LL JUST HAVE NORMAL RED BEAN.
OOH, DOES THIS ONE HAVE MOCHI IN IT?

I HEARD THAT IN THE OLD DAYS, IF YOU DID POORLY ON FINALS IN A MUSIC SCHOOL...
YOU'D GET THROWN OUT!
MUNCH
GUESS THAT'S HOW THEY WEEDED OUT THE WEAK-LINGS.
THAT'S HORRIBLE! I'M GLAD THEY DON'T DO *THAT* ANYMORE.
HEY, AI-CHAN, WHAT RANK WERE YOU ON EXAMS?
TWENTY-FOUR.
I WENT DOWN.
SO, RIGHT IN THE MIDDLE, HUH?
YEAH.
BUT I'M GONNA DO BETTER NEXT TIME.
I'M GONNA GET SERIOUS.

SO, YOU WEREN'T TAKING THIS SERI-OUSLY BEFORE?

IF ONLY YOU'D BEEN SERIOUS BACK IN JPX!
YOU'D BE THE TOP STAR BY NOW!

YEAH, I'M GETTING SERIOUS.
I FINALLY FOUND SOME-THING I WANT TO DO.

TO DO THAT...

I NEED TO AIM FOR THE TOP.

ONE DAY...
I WILL BE THE TOP STAR OF THE KOUKA TROUPE.

I KNOW...
I SHOULDN'T COMPARE MYSELF TO HER.
MIIIN
MIIIIN
NARATA-SAN'S ON A WHOLE OTHER LEVEL THAN I AM.
STILL...
I...
IF I HOLD OUT A LITTLE LONGER...
MIIN
MIIN

HIT THAT FALSETTO! OPEN THAT THROAT AND LET THAT VOICE RING OUT!

DRAW IT OUT!

HOLD IT!

HOOOLD IT!

Chapter 14

AHAAAAAA!

AHAAAAAAA!
AH...
COUGH!
COUGH!

YAMADA-SAN, I'M WORRIED.

ARE YOU SURE YOU'RE FEELING ALL RIGHT?
IS SOMETHING WRONG?

SORRY. I'M OKAY.

SHE'S SORRY, ALL RIGHT.
MUTTER

14

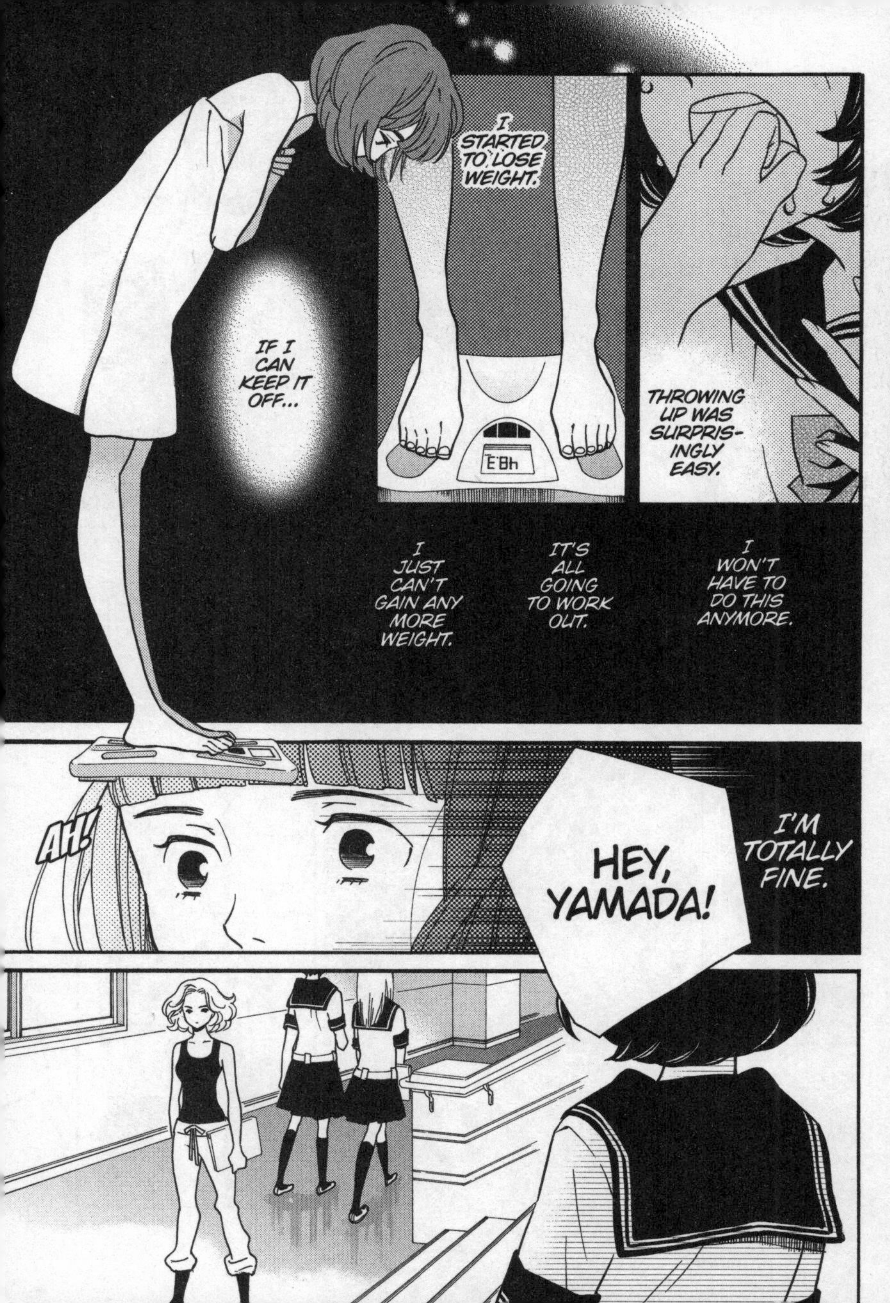
THROWING UP WAS SURPRIS-INGLY EASY.
I STARTED TO LOSE WEIGHT.
IF I CAN KEEP IT OFF...
I WON'T HAVE TO DO THIS ANYMORE.
IT'S ALL GOING TO WORK OUT.
I JUST CAN'T GAIN ANY MORE WEIGHT.
I'M TOTALLY FINE.
HEY, YAMADA!
AH!

HAVE YOU LOST WEIGHT?
Y-YES!

ABOUT FIVE KILO-GRAMS.
IS THAT SO?

DON'T HURT YOUR-SELF.
I WANT A DAILY REPORT OF WHAT YOU ATE AND WHEN, OKAY?

OKAY.
TACHI-BANA-SENSEI IS KINDA SCARY!
SHH!

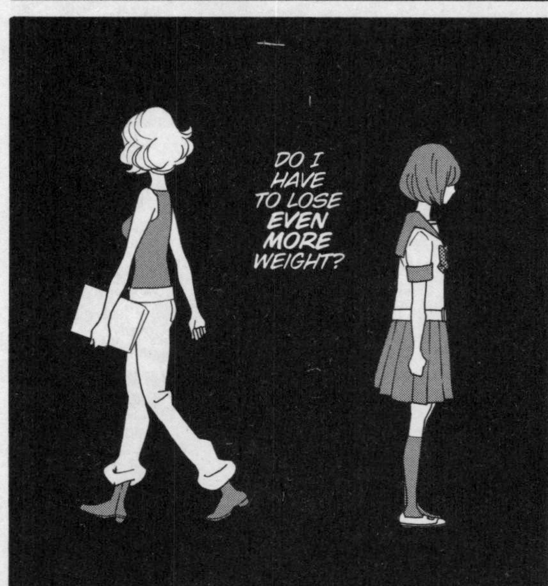
DO I HAVE TO LOSE EVEN MORE WEIGHT?

YO, TACHIBANA-SENSEI?
WHAT ARE YOU STEWING OVER?
IT'S ABOUT YAMADA AYAKO.
I THINK SHE MIGHT BE BULIMIC.

YAMADA...? OH, THE FIRST-YEAR IN CLASS A!
SHE *HAS* LOST A BIT OF WEIGHT RECENTLY.
YEAH, IT'S TRUE.

COME TO THINK OF IT, HER FINGERS WERE RED. SHE SAID IT WAS A MOSQUITO BITE...
BUT IT MIGHT BE FROM MAKING HERSELF VOMIT.
I HOPE THIS IS JUST A RUMOR...
BUT I HEARD YOU CALLED HER A "FATTY," TACHIBANA-SENSEI.
I DID.

GOOD GOD! WHAT KIND OF TEACHER ARE YOU, TACHIBANA-SENSEI?!
THESE ARE TEENAGE GIRLS! EVERY HARSH WORD HITS HOME!
YOU HAVE TO BE CAREFUL WHAT YOU SAY!
DON'T YOU CARE AT ALL?!
I DON'T SEE THE PROB-LEM.
THERE ARE PLENTY OF SOFT, KIND TEACHERS HERE AT THIS SCHOOL... LIKE *YOU*, ONODERA-SENSEI.
BUT WHEN THESE GIRLS GRADUATE AND JOIN THE TROUPE, THEY'RE GOING TO BE SUBJECTED TO A LOT OF HARSH RUMORS AND CRITICISM.
NO MATTER HOW POPULAR YOU GET, THERE WILL ALWAYS BE CRITICS.
I'D SAY *NOT* BEING HARSH ON THEM IS CRUELER.
YOU CAN'T BE WEAK IN SHOW BUSINESS.
THEY NEED TO TOUGHEN THEIR SKIN EARLY--THAT MEANS *NOW*.
SURE, BUT... YAMADA'S ESPE-CIALLY FRAGILE.

IF SHE QUITS, THAT'S JUST PROOF SHE WAS NEVER GOING TO MAKE IT.
I'M SORRY, BUT IT'S THE TRUTH.
IN ANY CASE...
WE NEED TO GET HER TO QUIT VOMITING UP HER MEALS.
First-Year, Class A Yamada Ayako
Yesterday:
Breakfast: Calorie bar, yogurt
Lunch: RA bento, orange juice
Dinner: RA dinner (salad, curry, and rice)
CRISPY CHIPS
SO GOOD!

COUGH!
ゲホッ
COUGH!
ゲホッ
ゲホ
COUGH!
NO, NO!
I CAN'T THROW UP.
I'LL GET FAT AGAIN.
I CAN'T LET THAT HAP-PEN.
SHWF
スッ
NCH
ビクッ

N-NARATA-SAN?! WHAT ARE YOU DOING?!
WHAT AM I DOING? THIS IS A BATH-ROOM. I HAD TO PEE.
RIGHT HERE...
IN THE MIDDLE...
OF...
YOUR BACK.
IT HURTS, DOESN'T IT?
AND NOT...
BECAUSE YOU'VE BEEN WORKING OUT.

WHEN YOU VOMIT, YOU BRING UP STOMACH ACID.
AND THAT ACID BURNS YOUR ESOPHAGUS.

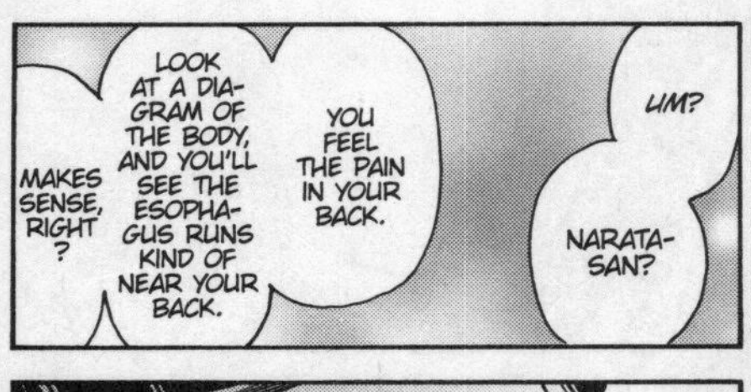
UM?
NARATA-SAN?
YOU FEEL THE PAIN IN YOUR BACK.
LOOK AT A DIAGRAM OF THE BODY, AND YOU'LL SEE THE ESOPHAGUS RUNS KIND OF NEAR YOUR BACK.
MAKES SENSE, RIGHT?

YOU GET DARK CIRCLES UNDER YOUR EYES.
YOU LOSE ENERGY, YOUR IMMUNE SYSTEM WEAKENS.

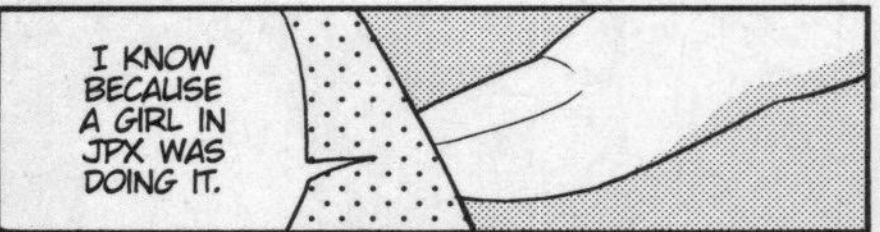
I KNOW BECAUSE A GIRL IN JPX WAS DOING IT.

SO...

SO WHAT?!

YOU MIGHT LOSE WEIGHT THIS WAY, BUT IT WON'T MAKE YOU PRETTIER.
......
I...
I DON'T WANT TO HEAR THAT.

NOT FROM SOMEONE WHO'S ALWAYS BEEN PRETTY!

C'MON, AYA! WAKE THE HELL UP ALREADY!
OH... MORNING.
MNGH!
WAIT, ARE YOU SICK WITH A COLD? IN THIS SUMMER HEAT?
I...I THINK I HAVE A FEVER...
YOU OKAY? STAYING HEALTHY IS PART OF OUR JOB, YOU KNOW!
SO, YOU GONNA STAY HERE OR WHAT?
NO. I'LL GO TO CLASS.
ALL RIGHT, GIRLS! WE'RE GOING TO DO SOMETHING SPECIAL TODAY. I WANT TO HEAR EVERYONE SING A SOLO.
SOMETIMES IT'S FUN TO MIX THINGS UP, RIGHT?
HEE HEE! ♡

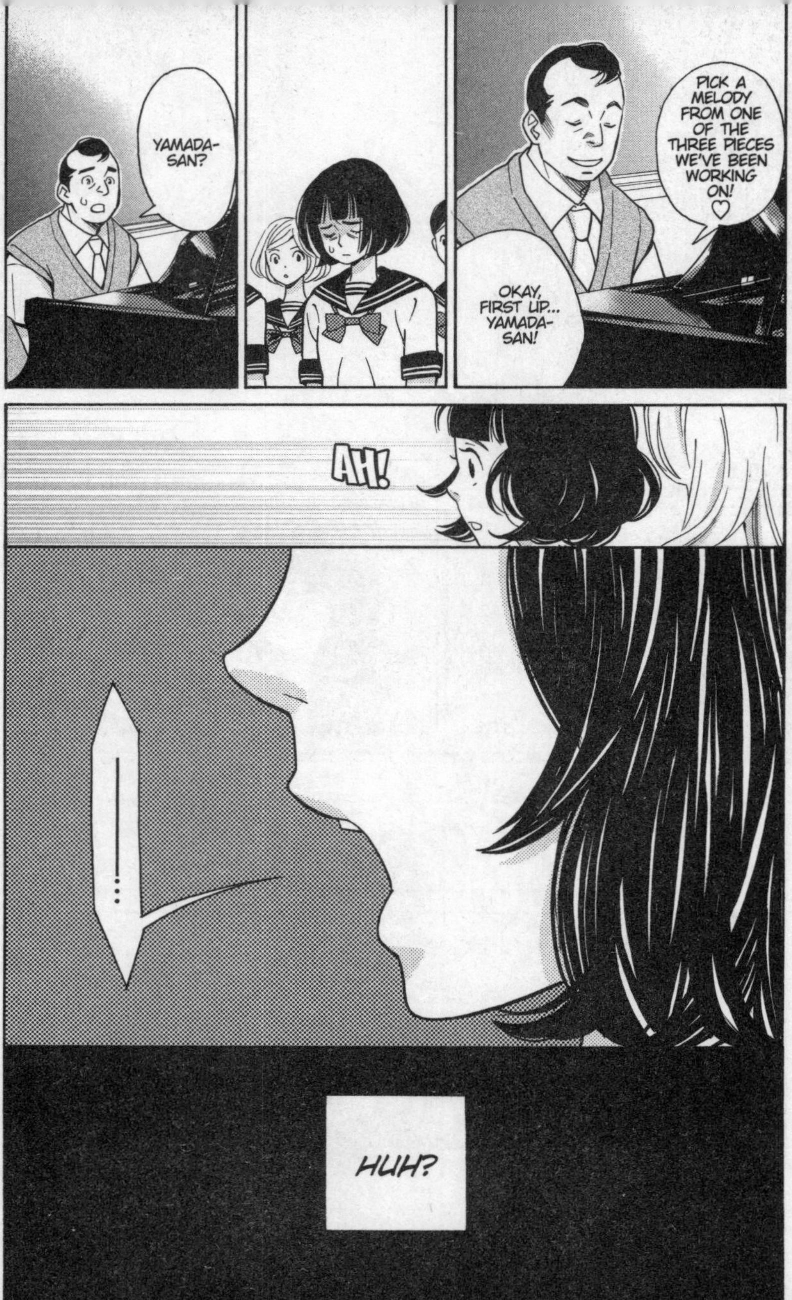

PICK A MELODY FROM ONE OF THE THREE PIECES WE'VE BEEN WORKING ON! ♡
OKAY, FIRST UP... YAMADA-SAN!

YAMADA-SAN?

AH!

…

HUH?

MY VOICE?!
I FEEL SO DIZZY.
I CAN'T EVEN STAND.
WHOA! YAMADA-SAN?!
LOOKS LIKE A STANDARD CASE OF PHARYNGITIS.
SINCE YOU HAVE A FEVER, I RECOMMEND A FEW DAYS OF REST.

UMM.
I'M A STU-DENT AT KOUKA.
WOW! YOU'RE GOING TO BE A BIG ACTRESS SOMEDAY, HM?
N-NO.
MY GRADES SUCK, AND I'M THIS CLOSE TO FAILING OUT.
I CAN'T REST.
I'LL GET LEFT IN THE DUST.
COULD YOU JUST GIVE ME SOME-THING...
TO HELP WITH MY FEVER?
MIIIN
MIIIN
"I WISH I COULD, BUT AS YOUR DOCTOR, I CAN'T RECOM-MEND THAT."
MIIIN

"WE DON'T WANT TO MAKE THINGS WORSE. IF YOUR THROAT SWELLS UP, YOU MIGHT NOT BE ABLE TO BREATHE."

NOW, REST UP.

OKAY?

JUST FOCUS ON GETTING BETTER.

FWUMF
MY BACK HURTS.

PING

You workin' hard?
A girl at my shop is a huge Kouka fan! She heard about you and was SO excited. Says she's rooting for you! Color me a proud big sis.

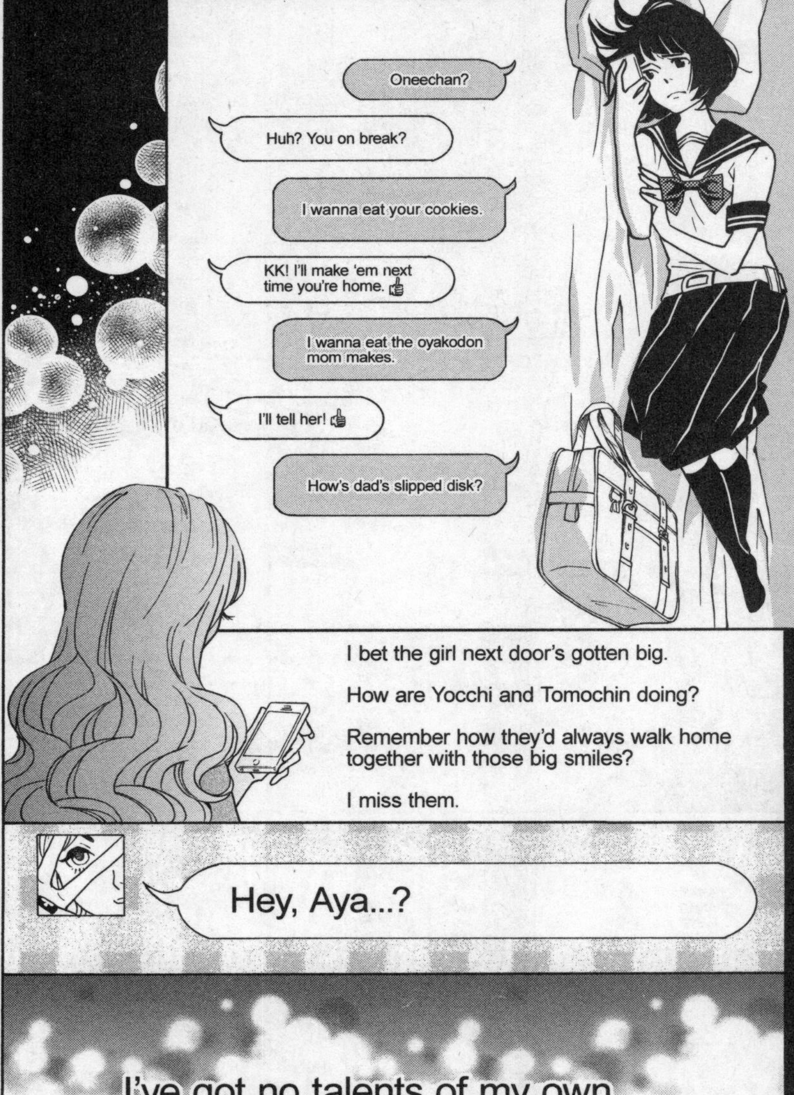
Oneechan?
Huh? You on break?
I wanna eat your cookies.
KK! I'll make 'em next time you're home.
I wanna eat the oyakodon mom makes.
I'll tell her!
How's dad's slipped disk?
I bet the girl next door's gotten big.
How are Yocchi and Tomochin doing?
Remember how they'd always walk home together with those big smiles?
I miss them.
Hey, Aya...?
I've got no talents of my own, so I can't say I understand your world too well.

But if you're suffering, or in pain, you can come home when-ever you want!!
I WANT TO GO BACK...
TO THE WORLD I KNEW BE-FORE.
I KNOW I WAS JUST CHASING IMPOSSIBLE DREAMS.
BUT...

I WAS HAPPY TO GET JUST A LITTLE BIT CLOSER TO THAT FANTASY WORLD.
BAM
BAM
YAMADA-SAN!
YOU'RE IN THERE, RIGHT?! CAN WE TALK?!
ONO-DERA-SEN-SEI!
YOU CAN'T BE IN HERE!
THIS IS AN EMERGENCY! PRETEND I'M NOT HERE!
MEN ARE NOT ALLOWED IN THE DORMS!
WELL, I'M A BEAUTIFUL KOUKA GIRL ON THE INSIDE!!
LISTEN.
YAMADA-SAN.

YOU'RE A KIND AND SENSITIVE GIRL.
I KNOW YOU PROBABLY KEEP ALL YOUR WORRIES TO YOURSELF.
BUT YOU'RE STILL SO YOUNG! YOUR PATH HASN'T BEEN SET IN STONE YET.
IT'S NORMAL TO FEEL LOST OR DISCOURAGED!

YOUR GRADES MIGHT BE BOTTOM OF THE BARREL...
BUT BELOW YOU ARE THE 1,095 GIRLS WHO DIDN'T MAKE IT INTO KOUKA AT ALL!
THE DOOR TO THE KOUKA THEATER TROUPE ONLY OPENS ONCE IN A LIFETIME FOR ITS CHOSEN YOUNG WOMEN.

ONCE YOU WALK OUT THAT DOOR, YOU CAN NEVER WALK THROUGH IT AGAIN.
I DON'T WANT YOU TO QUIT.
I KNOW IT FEELS LIKE YOUR DREAMS ARE SO FAR AWAY.
BUT KOUKA DOESN'T ADMIT JUST ANY GIRL, YOU KNOW!

DO YOU KNOW WHAT IT IS?
THAT SPECIAL TALENT OF YOURS?

......
SING-ING.

THAT'S RIGHT! SINGING!!
WHEN I HEARD YOUR VOICE DURING THE ADMISSION AUDITIONS, I *KNEW*!
I *KNEW* YOU WOULD BE THE NEXT GREAT *ETOILE** OF OUR TIME!!

**Etoile: The actress who sings the iconic solo at the beginning of the finale.*

I SEE YOU, THERE, IN THE GRAND FINALE OF THE GREATEST KOUKA SHOW...

STANDING CENTER STAGE ON THOSE STAIRS...
SINGING A CAPPELLA WITH THAT BEAUTIFUL VOICE OF YOURS!

ALL RIGHT, GIRLS!
LET'S START OUR WARM-UPS!
LET'S TURN TO PAGE--
KA-CHAK
SORRY!
SORRY I'M LATE!
YAMADA-SAN, ARE YOU FEELING BETTER?
YES! MY DOCTOR SAID I CAN START PRACTICING AGAIN.
GREAT! THEN WE'VE GOT EVERYONE HERE TODAY!
WHY DON'T WE PICK UP FROM WHERE WE LEFT OFF ON THOSE SOLOS, HUH?

RIGHT THEN, PICK ONE OF THOSE THREE SONGS...
AND LET'S HEAR YOUR COMEBACK SOLO, YAMADA-SAN!

OKAY.
OH, JEEZ! I'M SO NERVOUS!

The Rose
OH.
THIS IS THE SONG I SANG FOR MY AUDITION.

OKAY, YAMADA-SAN, LET'S GET GOING, SO EVERYONE GETS THEIR TURN!

IF I DON'T GIVE UP...
THEN IT'LL BE JUST AS ONODERA-SENSEI SAID.
I'LL STAND IN THE CENTER OF THOSE BIG KOUKA STAIRS AND SING.
NOBODY CAN SAY WHETHER THE DAY WILL COME...
WHEN THE AUDIENCE WILL APPLAUD ME AND ONLY ME.

OH, WOW! ♡ SHE HAS THE VOICE OF AN ANGEL!
I HAD NO IDEA AYA COULD SING LIKE THAT.
OH, I KNEW.

WE WERE IN THE SAME GROUP DURING AUDITIONS.
ONODERA-SENSEI LOOKED LIKE HE WAS ABOUT TO FALL ASLEEP, AND THEN, HE HEARD HER VOICE.

IT'S BEEN PISSING ME OFF THAT SHE HAS SO MUCH TALENT BUT ACTS SO TIMID.

THE ONLY THING I KNOW FOR SURE...
IS THAT IF I QUIT...
THEN MY DREAM REALLY WILL BE OVER.

THAT'S A QUOTE FROM SLAM DUNK, RIGHT?!
"IF I QUIT, THE GAME IS OVER!"
OH, YEAH. I GUESS IT IS.
I'M A HUGE MITCHI FAN! ♡
I LIKE RUKAWA.
YOU LOOK A LOT BETTER, YAMADA-SAN.
YEAH.
I'M SORRY I SAID THOSE MEAN THINGS TO YOU, NARATA-SAN.
IT'S FINE.
I WAS PRETTY BLUNT, TOO.
I'M NOT USED TO TALKING TO PEOPLE ABOUT STUFF LIKE THAT.

PEOPLE SAY I ACT LIKE A ROBOT.
THAT THEY CAN'T TELL WHAT I'M THINKING.
I NEED BE MORE EXPRESSIVE IF I WANT TO ACT, HUH?

WOW.
I DIDN'T KNOW NARATA-SAN HAD THINGS SHE WORRIED ABOUT.

YOUR SOPRANO VOICE WAS SO BEAUTIFUL, AYA-CHAN!
I WISH I COULD SING LIKE THAT!
BUT OSCAR IS A MALE ROLE, SO I CAN'T SING UP HIGH LIKE THAT ANYWAY.

WHEN DID YOU DECIDE YOU WANTED TO BE OSCAR, SARASA-CHAN?
WHEN I WAS LITTLE!
SO, IT'S BEEN A LIFE-LONG DREAM?
YUP! OH, WAIT!

Kageki Shojo!! The Curtain Rises / END

SPECIAL EXTRA:
A Day in the Life of a Kouka First-Year Student

CHAN.
SAN.
MIN
SAMA.
CCHI.
MIIIN
MIIIN
RIN.
PPE.
TAN.
MIIN
MIIIIN
WATANABE-SAN'S YOUNGER THAN ME.
MAYBE I SHOULD JUST USE "CHAN."

YAAAAWN! G'MORNING, AI-CHAN!
I HAVEN'T HAD A REAL FRIEND FOR MANY, MANY YEARS.
WOW! YOU'RE ALREADY IN YOUR UNIFORM?
......
I GOTTA GET READY, TOO!
AS SUCH, I'VE NEVER HAD THE CHANCE TO CALL SOMEONE BY A NICK-NAME.
MORNING...
SA...
WATANABE-SAN.
UGH, I'M SO BAD AT THIS.

AND THUS, THE FIRST-YEARS' DAY AT KOUKA BEGINS.
7:30 A.M.: MORNING CLEANING.
HUH?
HOW TO PICK A NICKNAME FOR SOME-ONE?
YOU CAN CALL ME "HIJIRI-SENPAI" WHENEVER YOU LIKE, YOU KNOW.
I KNOW.
I'M JUST BAD AT THAT SORT OF THING.
I'M SURPRISED YOU CAN CALL NOJINO-SENPAI AND NAKA-YAMA-SENPAI BY THEIR GIVEN NAMES...
ESPECIALLY SINCE YOU GUYS DON'T GET ALONG.
IT'S KINDA INCREDI-BLE.
......
WELL!
YOU'RE RIGHT.
WE DON'T GET ALONG, BUT WE STILL CALL EACH OTHER BY OUR GIVEN NAMES OR NICKNAMES.
LIKELY BECAUSE EVERYONE ELSE DOES, TOO.

WELL, IT DOESN'T REALLY MATTER.
NICK-NAMES DON'T MEAN ANY-THING.
CRACK
NICK-NAMES DO MATTER!
BUT EVEN IF I HATED SOME-ONE...
OH! BUT IT'S NOT LIKE I HATE RISA, OKAY?
ANYWAY, I WOULDN'T JUST PUT IT OUT IN THE OPEN THAT I DISLIKE THEM.
WAIT, DIDN'T YOU ALL HAVE NICKNAMES BACK IN JPX48, NARATA-SAN?
NOD
IN THE IDOL GROUP JPX48...

THERE WAS A RULE THAT YOU HAD TO CALL EACH OTHER BY YOUR NICKNAMES.
BING
BONG
YOUR NICKNAME WAS BASICALLY YOUR STAGE NAME, SO...
BENG
BONG
CLAMOR
わぁ
CLAMOR
わぁ
CLAMOR
わぁ
CLAMOR
わぁ
WE HAVE DOUBLE BALLET TODAY!
SHOOT!
I LEFT MY LEOTARD IN THE DRYER!
MINE'S STINKY! OH GOD, I'M GONNA STINK!
DON'T WORRY, IT'S SUMMER. WE'RE ALL GONNA BE SWEATY AND SMELLY SOON!
9 A.M.: CLASS STARTS.
ONE.
TWO.
THREE.
ONE.
TWO.
THREE.
THE KOUKA SCHOOL SCHED-ULE...
IS DIVIDED INTO TWO MORNING PERIODS AND THREE AFTERNOON PERIODS.

ALL THE BREAKS BETWEEN CLASSES ARE FOR CHANGING CLOTHES OR MOVING BETWEEN CLASSROOMS.
OKAY, AND NEXT!
AS SUCH, STUDENTS DON'T TALK TO EACH OTHER MUCH WHEN ON SCHOOL GROUNDS.
ONE.
TWO.
THREE.
I'LL START WITH "SARASA-CHAN."
THEN I'LL TRY A NICKNAME.
I HAVEN'T CALLED SOMEONE BY A NICKNAME SINCE ELEMENTARY SCHOOL...
IF I START CALLING HER "SARASA-CHAN"...
WILL PEOPLE...
BE WEIRDED OUT?

WHOA, "CHAN" IS WAY TOO CASUAL!
UGH! NOW I CAN ONLY IMAGINE THE WORST-CASE SCENARIO.
IS SHE THAT THIRSTY TO BE FRIENDS?
WHAT A DOLT, RIGHT?!
YOU CAN'T JUST APPROACH ME LIKE THEY DO IN JOJO'S!
YOU'VE SAID A WHOLE LOTTA MEAN THINGS TO ME, YOU KNOW!
IF THIS WERE THE ROSE OF VERSAILLES...
YOU'D BE THE MARQUIS DE BOUILLÉ!
ARGH! I KEEP MAKING HER EVEN MEANER IN MY HEAD!
NARATA-SAN! FOCUS!

BING
BONG
BENG...
11:30 A.M.: FIFTY-MINUTE LUNCH PERIOD.
WHAT'S UP, AI-CHAN? YOU'RE NOT EATING.
......
SARA-SA.
SA...
WA...
TANABE-SAN.
SARA-SA.
I'M NOT THAT HUNGRY TODAY.
SLUMP...

THAT'S NOT OKAY, NARATA-SAN! YOU HAVE TO EAT.
YOU NEED YOUR ENERGY FOR AFTER-NOON CLASSES.
BALLET, DRAMA, THEN TAP!
THAT'S GONNA USE A LOT OF ENERGY!
THOUGH WE CAN SAVE A LITTLE ENERGY IN DRAMA 'CAUSE WE'RE JUST REVIEWING THEORY.
WHAT? YOU GUYS TIRED? SLEEPY?
TAKE A NAP IF YOU WANT! I WON'T WAKE YA.
THE WAY THE PHANTOM SMILES WHILE HE RATTLES OFF ALL YOUR MISTAKES, THOUGH...
IT'S DEMONIC!
I FEEL YA. I DON'T LIKE SUMMER.
IT'S TOUGH TO EAT WHEN IT'S THIS HOT OUT.

YOU MENTIONED BEFORE THAT YOU DON'T LIKE SUMMER.
YEAH! I DUNNO WHY, BUT SUMMER ALWAYS MAKES ME FEEL SO SAD.
MIIN
MIIN
SAD IN THE SUMMER? NOT THE WINTER?
MIIN
SPEAKING OF SUMMER...
NOM NOM
SUMMER VACATION STARTS NEXT MONTH, RIGHT?
WHAT'S EVERYONE GONNA DO?
GO BACK HOME?
WE'RE GOING BACK HOME TO HOKKAI-DO!
SUMMER'S NOT SO BAD UP NORTH.
I'M GOING HOME, TOO.
SAME, UP TO KANAGAWA.
I'M GOING BACK TO TOKYO! MY GRANDPA REALLY MISSES ME.
YOUR FAMILY'S IN TOKYO TOO, RIGHT, AI-CHAN?
YEAH.
BUT...

I'M NOT GOING HOME.
NOBODY THERE MISSES ME.
AND EVEN IF I WENT BACK TO TOKYO, I'D JUST HANG OUT AT TAICHI'S PLACE OR HIS STUDIO.
SO, I'LL JUST STAY HERE AT THE DORM.
BUT WHY?!
IT'S SUMMER BREAK!
IS YOUR FAMILY NOT HOME OR SOMETHING?
AGH!
READ BETWEEN THE LINES, GIRL!
MAYBE HER FAMILY SITUATION'S COMPLICATED!
OH, I KNOW!

IF NOBODY'S WAITING FOR YOU AT HOME...
THEN YOU CAN STAY OVER AT MY PLACE, AI-CHAN!
HUH?
I CAN ...?
OF COURSE! IT'S GONNA BE SO MUCH FUN! ♡
WHOA !!
THIS IS... REALLY LIKE...
LIKE WE'RE FRIENDS !
I...
I'VE NEVER STAYED OVER AT A FRIEND'S BEFORE.
REALLY?

12:40 P.M.: BALLET.
WOW!
I FEEL LIKE...
2:10 P.M.: DRAMA.
I'VE UNLOCKED THE TOP LEVEL OF FRIEND-SHIP...
YOU'RE SCARING ME, NARATA.
GLARE
GLARE
IN ONE FELL SWOOP!
3:40 P.M.: TAP DANCE.
TAAAAAP!
WHO CARES WHAT I CALL HER NOW!

AFTER VARIOUS OTHER LESSONS, THEIR DAY ENDS AT AROUND 7 P.M., AND THEY HEAD HOME.
I'M POOPED!
I'M STARVING!
WHAT'S ON THE MENU FOR TODAY?
I HOPE IT'S CURRY!
SUMMER BREAK'S IN AUGUST.
AUGUST.
I WANT TONKATSU!
I'LL SPEND AUGUST...
AT SARASA'S HOUSE.
MURMUR
WHAT?
I HEARD YOU!
YOU JUST CALLED ME "SARASA"!!

I DID NOT!
TURN
I HEARD YOU!
WHY'D YOU SAY IT? YOU CAN TOTALLY CALL ME SARASA, YOU KNOW!
YOU'RE WRONG!
I DIDN'T SAY IT!
TMP
TMP
THAT MAKES US FRIENDS!
FRIENDS...
F... FINE.
I'LL JUST CALL YOU SARASA FROM NOW ON.
KOUKA

Bonus Manga #1
THE WEATHER'S SO NICE!
I THINK THIS IS THE FIRST TIME WE'VE BEEN OUT SOME-WHERE AS A GROUP.
BE KOBE

YEAH, USUALLY WHEN WE'RE TOGETHER, WE'RE IN CLASS OR PRACTICING.
RIGHT! WE'VE NEVER HUNG OUT OUTSIDE OF SCHOOL LIKE THIS.

I'VE BEEN HERE BEFORE!
SAME.
OH, YEAH! BACK WHEN NARACCHI DITCHED CLASS!
GOD, RIGHT? WE ALMOST ALL GOT IN TROUBLE OVER THAT!
HEY, IT'S ALL IN THE PAST NOW!
I'M JUST GLAD AI-CHAN WAS OKAY!

I'M SORRY.
I KNOW I MADE SARASA AND ALL OF YOU WORRY.

NOTHING.
I JUST NOTICED YOU'RE CALLING HER "SARASA" NOW!
GAUZE TOP
WELL.
WE'RE FRIENDS.
URK!
NOW I FEEL WEIRD DOING IT.
IT IS OKAY, RIGHT?
HOSHINO-SAN!
SHE'S FINALLY COME OUT OF HER SHELL! DON'T SCARE HER BACK INTO IT!
HMM.
SO...
WE'RE CALLING OUR FRIENDS BY THEIR GIVEN NAMES?
IF YOU'RE NOT USING MY GIVEN NAME...
DOES THAT MEAN WE'RE NOT FRIENDS?

HO...
HOSHI...
KA...
KA...
KA...
KA...
KAORU.
FIDGET
FIDGET
WOW.
SO YOU CAN SAY IT.
FIDGET

I CAN SAY IT, TOO!
KAORU...
CHAN!
KA... KAORU... CHAN...
GAUZE TOR
WAIT!
YOU KNOW WHAT WOULD BE EVEN TRUER TO MY BRAND? USING "-KUN" INSTEAD OF "-CHAN"! DOESN'T THAT GET YOUR HEART RACING?!
YOU WANNA BE AN OTOKOYAKU, RIGHT, KAORU-CHAN? IF SO, THERE'S A TEENY, TINY CHANCE YOU MIGHT PLAY A CHARACTER...
IN AN EVAN-GEL--
OOOH, OR WE COULD PUT IT IN KATAKANA AND SING IT TO THE TUNE OF BEETHOVEN'S NINTH! THAT WOULD BE PERFECT!
OKAY, YOU KNOW WHAT? JUST CALL ME "HOSHINO."
KA...
END

Bonus Manga #2
IMPORTANT ANNOUNCEMENT, EVERYONE!
PLEASE LISTEN UP!
WHAT'S WITH HER?
I'VE GOT A BAD FEELING ABOUT THIS!
KOBE

THIS ISN'T ACTUALLY KOBE.
WE EXIST IN A DIMENSION BETWEEN 2D AND 3D!
WHAT ARE YOU TALKING ABOUT?
SO... 2.5D?
STAGE ADAPTATIONS OF MANGA ARE 2.5D, RIGHT?
SO, THERE ARE A BUNCH OF 2.5D KOUKA SHOWS?
THAT'S NOT WHAT I MEAN!
THE WORLD OF KAGEKI SHOJO!!
WE ARE HERE!!
THE READER'S UNIVERSE
RIGHT NOW, WE EXIST BETWEEN OUR WORLD AND THE READER'S WORLD!
UM? WHAT?
I DON'T GET IT.
IT MAKES NO SENSE.
SHE'S BEING WEIRDER THAN USUAL.
......
COO COO
I GET IT!
YOU DO?!

OKAY THEN, DEAR READERS!
DEAR READERS?
AI ETACHED ERSELF MOTION-ALLY FROM EVERY-THING.
LOOK AT MY DESK IN THIS PANEL!
BAM
MY FAMILY RUNS A TATAMI FLOORING BUSINESS...
SO, MY ROOM IS NEVER CLUTTERED OR MESSY!
疊渡邊
THE PERSON WHO MADE THIS MESS WASN'T ME, IT WAS THE AUTHOR!
Sign: Watanabe Tatami
THEN, WE HAVE AI-CHAN'S BANGS!
FWIP
Before
open
THE DESIGN CHANGED PARTWAY THROUGH THE MANGA!
After
closed
DID YOU NOTICE THAT, DEAR READERS?

IT WAS CHANGED BECAUSE THE AUTHOR DECIDED DRAWING IT THAT WAY WAS EASIER!
IT ALSO MADE IT EASIER FOR HER ASSISTANTS TO APPLY SCREEN TONES!
IF YOU KEEP ACTING WEIRD LIKE THIS, I'M JUST GOING TO CALL YOU "WATA-NABE-SAN" FROM NOW ON.
SAME.
DITTO!
WE'RE HEADING BACK... WATA-NABE-SAN.
EH?
NO!
PLEASE, WAIT!
NOT YOU TOO, SUGIMOTO-SAN!
WHAT?
IS SHE JUST MAKING EXCUSES FOR SOME-THING, OR...?
FREAKY!
......
OH!
AI-CHAN!
NOD
I'M HEADING BACK TOO...
WATANABE-SAN.
BOOM

HAUGH!
WHAT'S UP, SARA-SA?
JOLT
SA... RASA?
IT WAS A DREAM?
"IT WAS ALL A DREAM"? THAT'S A PRETTY CLICHÉ TWIST.
HOW BORING.
DON'T YOU AGREE?
BOY, WAS THAT A CRAZY DREAM!
MORE LIKE A NIGHT-MARE! I'M SO GLAD IT WASN'T REAL!
HUNH.
?!
WHO ARE YOU TALKING TO, AI-CHAN?! WHO?!
END

Thank you so much for reading
Kageki Shojo!! The Curtain Rises.

This prequel to *Kageki Shojo!!* was serialized in a magazine that doesn't exist anymore (*Jump X*), so I want to extend a big thanks to the staff of the magazine and Hakusensha for working hard to get it published!

Ai-chan's idol group JPX48 is based off the name of that magazine (*Jump X*).

I plan on continuing the main series in Hakusensha's *Melody* magazine and developing the story of our heroine, Sarasa!

Thank you all for reading my work.

With love,
Kumiko Saiki

SEVEN SEAS ENTERTAINMENT PRESENTS

KAGEKI SHOJO!!
The Curtain Rises

story and art by **KUMIKO SAIKI**

TRANSLATION
Katrina Leonoudakis

LETTERING AND RETOUCH
Laura Heo

COVER DESIGN
(LOGO) Courtney Williams
KC Fabellon

PROOFREADER
Rebecca Schnedidereit

EDITOR
Shannon Fay

PREPRESS TECHNICIAN
Rhiannon Rasmussen-Silverstein

PRODUCTION MANAGER
Lissa Pattillo

MANAGING EDITOR
Julie Davis

ASSOCIATE PUBLISHER
Adam Arnold

PUBLISHER
Jason DeAngelis

KAGEKI SHOJO!! SEASON ZERO
BY KUMIKO SAIKI

First published in Japan in 2019 by HAKUSENSHA, INC., Tokyo.
English language translation rights in U.S.A. arranged with HAKUSENSHA, INC., Tokyo through TOHAN CORPORATION, Tokyo.

Seven Seas press and purchase enquiries can be sent to Marketing Manager Lianne Sentar at press@gomanga.com. Information regarding the distribution and purchase of digital editions is available from Digital Manager CK Russell at digital@gomanga.com.

ISBN: 978-1-64505-835-9

Printed in Canada

First Printing: November 2020

10 9 8 7 6 5 4 3 2 1

FOLLOW US ONLINE: ***www.sevenseasentertainment.com***

READING DIRECTIONS

This book reads from ***right to left***, Japanese style. If this is your first time reading manga, you start reading from the top right panel on each page and take it from there. If you get lost, just follow the numbered diagram here. It may seem backwards at first, but you'll get the hang of it! Have fun!!

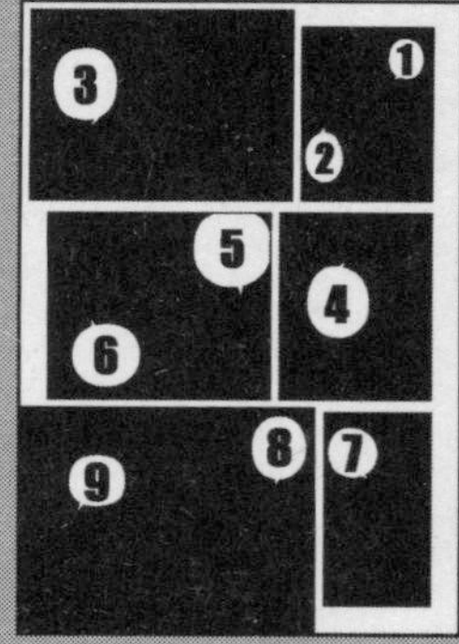